NON SANS DROICT.

William Shakespeare

THE TEMPEST

Edited by Robert Langbaum

GENERAL EDITOR: SYLVAN BARNET
The Signet Classic Shakespeare

A SIGNET CLASSIC
NEW AMERICAN LIBRARY
TIMES MIRROR
NEW YORK AND SCARBOROUGH, ONTARIO
THE NEW ENGLISH LIBRARY LIMITED, LONDON

SIGNET, SIGNET CLASSICS, MENTOR, PLUME AND MERIDIAN BOOKS
are published *in the United States* by
The New American Library, Inc.,
1301 Avenue of the Americas, New York, New York 10019,
in Canada by The New American Library of Canada Limited,
81 Mack Avenue, Scarborough, 704, Ontario,
in the United Kingdom by The New English Library Limited,
Barnard's Inn, Holborn, London, E.C. 1, England

11 12 13 14 15 16 17 18

PRINTED IN THE UNITED STATES OF AMERICA

Contents

Shakespeare: Prefatory Remarks

Between the record of his baptism in Stratford on 26 April 1564 and the record of his burial in Stratford on 25 April 1616, some forty documents name Shakespeare, and many others name his parents, his children, and his grandchildren. More facts are known about William Shakespeare than about any other playwright of the period except Ben Jonson. The facts should, however, be distinguished from the legends. The latter, inevitably more engaging and better known, tell us that the Stratford boy killed a calf in high style, poached deer and rabbits, and was forced to flee to London, where he held horses outside a playhouse. These traditions are only traditions; they may be true, but no evidence supports them, and it is well to stick to the facts.

Mary Arden, the dramatist's mother, was the daughter of a substantial landowner; about 1557 she married John Shakespeare, who was a glove-maker and trader in various farm commodities. In 1557 John Shakespeare was a member of the Council (the governing body of Stratford), in 1558 a constable of the borough, in 1561 one of the two town chamberlains, in 1565 an alderman (entitling him to the appellation "Mr."), in 1568 high bailiff—the town's highest political office, equivalent to mayor. After 1577, for an unknown reason he drops out of local politics. The birthday of William Shakespeare, the eldest son of this locally prominent man, is unrecorded; but the Stratford parish register records that the infant was baptized on 26 April 1564. (It is quite possible that he was born on 23 April, but this date has probably been assigned by tradition because it is the date on which, fifty-two years later, he died.) The attendance records of ·the Stratford grammar school of the period are not extant, but it is reasonable to assume that the son of a local official attended the school and received substantial training in Latin. The masters of the school from Shakespeare's seventh to fifteenth years held Oxford degrees; the Elizabethan curriculum excluded mathematics and the natural sciences but taught a good deal of Latin rhetoric, logic, and literature. On 27 November 1582 a marriage license was issued to Shakespeare and Anne Hathaway, eight years his senior. The couple had a child in May, 1583. Perhaps the marriage was necessary, but perhaps the couple had earlier engaged in a formal "troth plight" which would render their children legitimate even if no further ceremony were performed. In 1585 Anne Hathaway bore Shakespeare twins.

That Shakespeare was born is excellent; that he married and had children is pleasant; but that we know nothing about his departure from Stratford to London, or about the beginning of his theatrical career, is lamentable and must be admitted. We would gladly sacrifice details about his children's baptism for details about his earliest days on the stage. Perhaps the poaching episode is true (but it is first reported almost a century after Shakespeare's death), or perhaps he first left Stratford to be a schoolteacher, as another tradition holds; perhaps he was moved by

> Such wind as scatters young men through the world,
> To seek their fortunes further than at home
> Where small experience grows.

In 1592, thanks to the cantankerousness of Robert Greene, a rival playwright and a pamphleteer, we have our first reference, a snarling one, to Shakespeare as an actor and playwright. Greene warns those of his own educated friends who wrote for the theater against an actor who has presumed to turn playwright:

> There is an upstart crow, beautified with our feathers, that with his *tiger's heart wrapped in a player's hide* supposes he is as well able to bombast out a blank verse as the best of

you, and being an absolute Johannes-factotum is in his own
conceit the only Shake-scene in a country.

The reference to the player, as well as the allusion to
Aesop's crow (who strutted in borrowed plumage, as an
actor struts in fine words not his own), makes it clear that
by this date Shakespeare had both acted and written. That
Shakespeare is meant is indicated not only by "Shake-
scene" but by the parody of a line from one of Shakespeare's plays, *3 Henry VI:* "O, tiger's heart wrapped in
a woman's hide." If Shakespeare in 1592 was prominent
enough to be attacked by an envious dramatist, he probably had served an apprenticeship in the theater for at least
a few years.

In any case, by 1592 Shakespeare had acted and written,
and there are a number of subsequent references to him as
an actor: documents indicate that in 1598 he is a "principal
comedian," in 1603 a "principal tragedian," in 1608 he is
one of the "men players." The profession of actor was not
for a gentleman, and it occasionally drew the scorn of
university men who resented writing speeches for persons
less educated than themselves, but it was respectable
enough: players, if prosperous, were in effect members of
the bourgeoisie, and there is nothing to suggest that Stratford considered William Shakespeare less than a solid citizen. When, in 1596, the Shakespeares were granted a coat
of arms, the grant was made to Shakespeare's father, but
probably William Shakespeare (who the next year bought
the second-largest house in town) had arranged the matter
on his own behalf. In subsequent transactions he is occasionally styled a gentleman.

Although in 1593 and 1594 Shakespeare published two
narrative poems dedicated to the Earl of Southampton,
Venus and Adonis and *The Rape of Lucrece,* and may well
have written most or all of his sonnets in the middle nine-
ties, Shakespeare's literary activity seems to have been almost entirely devoted to the theater. (It may be significant
that the two narrative poems were written in years when
the plague closed the theaters for several months.) In 1594
he was a charter member of a theatrical company called the

Chamberlain's Men (which in 1603 changed its name to the King's Men); until he retired to Stratford (about 1611, apparently), he was with this remarkably stable company. From 1599 the company acted primarily at the Globe Theatre, in which Shakespeare held a one-tenth interest. Other Elizabethan dramatists are known to have acted, but no other is known also to have been entitled to a share in the profits of the playhouse.

Shakespeare's first eight published plays did not have his name on them, but this is not remarkable; the most popular play of the sixteenth century, Thomas Kyd's *The Spanish Tragedy,* went through many editions without naming Kyd, and Kyd's authorship is known only because a book on the profession of acting happens to quote (and attribute to Kyd) some lines on the interest of Roman emperors in the drama. What is remarkable is that after 1598 Shakespeare's name commonly appears on printed plays—some of which are not his. Another indication of his popularity comes from Francis Meres, author of *Palladis Tamia: Wit's Treasury* (1598): in this anthology of snippets accompanied by an essay on literature, many playwrights are mentioned, but Shakespeare's name occurs more often than any other, and Shakespeare is the only playwright whose plays are listed.

From his acting, playwriting, and share in a theater, Shakespeare seems to have made considerable money. He put it to work, making substantial investments in Stratford real estate. When he made his will (less than a month before he died), he sought to leave his property intact to his descendants. Of small bequests to relatives and to friends (including three actors, Richard Burbage, John Heminges, and Henry Condell), that to his wife of the second-best bed has provoked the most comment; perhaps it was the bed the couple had slept in, the best being reserved for visitors. In any case, had Shakespeare not excepted it, the bed would have gone (with the rest of his household possessions) to his daughter and her husband. On 25 April 1616 he was buried within the chancel of the church at Stratford. An unattractive monument to his memory, placed on a wall near the grave, says he died on 23 April. Over the grave itself are the lines, perhaps by Shakespeare, that (more than his literary fame) have kept his bones undisturbed in the crowded burial ground where old bones were often dislodged to make way for new:

> Good friend, for Jesus' sake forbear
> To dig the dust enclosed here.
> Blessed be the man that spares these stones
> And cursed be he that moves my bones.

Thirty-seven plays, as well as some nondramatic poems, are held to constitute the Shakespeare canon. The dates of composition of most of the works are highly uncertain, but there is often evidence of a *terminus a quo* (starting point) and/or a *terminus ad quem* (terminal point) that provides a framework for intelligent guessing. For example, *Richard II* cannot be earlier than 1595, the publication date of some material to which it is indebted; *The Merchant of Venice* cannot be later than 1598, the year Francis Meres mentioned it. Sometimes arguments for a date hang on an alleged topical allusion, such as the lines about the unseasonable weather in *A Midsummer Night's Dream,* II.i.81—117, but such an allusion (if indeed it is an allusion) can be variously interpreted, and in any case there is always the possibility that a topical allusion was inserted during a revision, years after the composition of a play. Dates are often attributed on the basis of style, and although conjectures about style usually rest on other conjectures, sooner or later one must rely on one's literary sense. There is no real proof, for example, that *Othello* is not as early as *Romeo and Juliet,* but one feels *Othello* is later, and because the first record of its performance is 1604, one is glad enough to set its composition at that date and not push it back into Shakespeare's early years. The following chronology, then, is as much indebted to informed guesswork and sensitivity as it is to fact. The dates, necessarily imprecise, indicate something like a scholarly consensus.

PLAYS

1588–93   *The Comedy of Errors*

1588–94	Love's Labor's Lost
1590–91	2 Henry VI
1590–91	3 Henry VI
1591–92	1 Henry VI
1592–93	Richard III
1592–94	Titus Andronicus
1593–94	The Taming of the Shrew
1593–95	The Two Gentlemen of Verona
1594–96	Romeo and Juliet
1595	Richard II
1594–96	A Midsummer Night's Dream
1596–97	King John
1596–97	The Merchant of Venice
1597	1 Henry IV
1597–98	2 Henry IV
1598–1600	Much Ado About Nothing
1598–99	Henry V
1599	Julius Caesar
1599–1600	As You Like It
1599–1600	Twelfth Night
1600–01	Hamlet
1597–1601	The Merry Wives of Windsor
1601–02	Troilus and Cressida
1602–04	All's Well That Ends Well
1603–04	Othello
1604	Measure for Measure
1605–06	King Lear
1605–06	Macbeth
1606–07	Antony and Cleopatra
1605–08	Timon of Athens
1607–09	Coriolanus
1608–09	Pericles
1609–10	Cymbeline
1610–11	The Winter's Tale
1611	The Tempest
1612–13	Henry VIII

POEMS

| 1592 | Venus and Adonis |

Shakespeare's Theater

In Shakespeare's infancy, Elizabethan actors performed wherever they could—in great halls, at court, in the court-yards of inns. The innyards must have made rather unsatisfactory theaters: on some days they were unavailable because carters bringing goods to London used them as depots; when available, they had to be rented from the innkeeper; perhaps most important, London inns were subject to the Common Council of London, which was not well disposed toward theatricals. In 1574 the Common Council required that plays and playing places in London be licensed. It asserted that

> sundry great disorders and inconveniences have been found to ensue to this city by the inordinate haunting of great multitudes of people, specially youth, to plays, interludes, and shows, namely occasion of frays and quarrels, evil practices of incontinency in great inns having chambers and secret places adjoining to their open stages and galleries,

and ordered that innkeepers who wished licenses to hold performances put up a bond and make contributions to the poor.

The requirement that plays and innyard theaters be licensed, along with the other drawbacks of playing at inns, probably drove James Burbage (a carpenter-turned-actor) to rent in 1576 a plot of land northeast of the city walls and to build here—on property outside the jurisdiction of the city—England's first permanent construction designed for plays. He called it simply the Theatre. About all that is known of its construction is that it was wood. It soon had imitators, the most famous being the Globe (1599), built across the Thames (again outside the city's jurisdiction), out of timbers of the Theatre, which had been dismantled when Burbage's lease ran out.

There are three important sources of information about the structure of Elizabethan playhouses—drawings, a contract, and stage directions in plays. Of drawings, only the so-called De Witt drawing (c. 1596) of the Swan—really a friend's copy of De Witt's drawing—is of much significance. It shows a building of three tiers, with a stage jutting from a wall into the yard or center of the building. The tiers are roofed, and part of the stage is covered by a roof that projects from the rear and is supported at its front on two posts, but the groundlings, who paid a penny to stand in front of the stage, were exposed to the sky. (Performances in such a playhouse were held only in the daytime; artificial illumination was not used.) At the rear of the stage are two doors; above the stage is a gallery. The second major source of information, the contract for the Fortune, specifies that although the Globe is to be the model, the Fortune is to be square, eighty feet outside and fifty-five inside. The stage is to be forty-three feet broad, and is to extend into the middle of the yard (i.e., it is twenty-seven and a half feet deep). For patrons willing to pay more than the general admission charged of the groundlings, there were to be three galleries provided with seats. From the third chief source, stage directions, one learns that entrance to the stage was by doors, presumably spaced widely apart at the rear ("Enter one citizen at one door, and another at the other"), and that in addition to the platform stage there was occasionally some sort of curtained booth or alcove allowing for "discovery" scenes, and some sort of playing space "aloft" or "above" to represent (for example) the top of a city's walls or a room above the street. Doubtless each theater had its own peculiarities, but perhaps we can talk about a "typical" Elizabethan theater if we realize that no theater need exactly have fit the description, just as no father is the typical father with 3.7 children. This hypothetical theater is wooden, round or polygonal (in *Henry V* Shakespeare calls it a "wooden *O*"), capable of holding some eight hundred spectators standing in the yard around the projecting elevated stage and some fifteen hundred additional spectators seated in the three roofed galleries. The stage, protected by a "shadow" or "heavens" or roof, is entered by two doors; behind the doors is the "tiring house" (attiring house, i.e., dressing room), and above the doors is some sort of gallery that may sometimes hold spectators but that can be used (for example) as the bedroom from which Romeo—according to a stage direction in one text—"goeth down." Some evidence suggests that a throne can be lowered onto the platform stage, perhaps from the "shadow"; certainly characters can descend from the stage through a trap or traps into the cellar or "hell." Sometimes this space beneath the platform accommodates a sound-effects man or musician (in *Antony and Cleopatra* "music of the hautboys is under the stage") or an actor (in *Hamlet* the "Ghost cries under the stage"). Most characters simply walk on and off, but because there is no curtain in front of the platform, corpses will have to be carried off (Hamlet must lug Polonius' guts into the neighbor room), or will have to fall at the rear, where the curtain on the alcove or booth can be drawn to conceal them.

Such may have been the so-called "public theater." Another kind of theater, called the "private theater" because its much greater admission charge limited its audience to the wealthy or the prodigal, must be briefly mentioned. The private theater was basically a large room, entirely roofed and therefore artificially illuminated, with a stage at one end. In 1576 one such theater was established in Blackfriars, a Dominican priory in London that had been suppressed in 1538 and confiscated by the Crown and thus was not under the city's jurisdiction. All the actors in the Blackfriars theater were boys about eight to thirteen years old (in the public theaters similar boys played female parts; a boy Lady Macbeth played to a man Macbeth). This private theater had a precarious existence, and ceased operations in 1584. In 1596 James Burbage, who had already made theatrical history by building the Theatre, began to construct a second Blackfriars theater. He died in 1597, and for several years this second Blackfriars theater was used by a troupe of boys, but in 1608 two of Burbage's sons and five other actors (including

Shakespeare) became joint operators of the theater, using it in the winter when the open-air Globe was unsuitable. Perhaps such a smaller theater, roofed, artificially illuminated, and with a tradition of a courtly audience, exerted an influence on Shakespeare's late plays.

Performances in the private theaters may well have had intermissions during which music was played, but in the public theaters the action was probably uninterrupted, flowing from scene to scene almost without a break. Actors would enter, speak, exit, and others would immediately enter and establish (if necessary) the new locale by a few properties and by words and gestures. Here are some samples of Shakespeare's scene painting:

> This is Illyria, lady.

> Well, this is the Forest of Arden.

> This castle hath a pleasant seat; the air
> Nimbly and sweetly recommends itself
> Unto our gentle senses.

On the other hand, it is a mistake to conceive of the Elizabethan stage as bare. Although Shakespeare's Chorus in *Henry V* calls the stage an "unworthy scaffold" and urges the spectators to "eke out our performance with your mind," there was considerable spectacle. The last act of *Macbeth,* for example, has five stage directions calling for "drum and colors," and another sort of appeal to the eye is indicated by the stage direction "Enter Macduff, with Macbeth's head." Some scenery and properties may have been substantial; doubtless a throne was used, and in one play of the period we encounter this direction: "Hector takes up a great piece of rock and casts at Ajax, who tears up a young tree by the roots and assails Hector." The matter is of some importance, and will be glanced at again in the next section.

The Texts of Shakespeare

Though eighteen of his plays were published during his

lifetime, Shakespeare seems never to have supervised their publication. There is nothing unusual here; when a playwright sold a play to a theatrical company he surrendered his ownership of it. Normally a company would not publish the play, because to publish it meant to allow competitors to acquire the piece. Some plays, however, did get published: apparently treacherous actors sometimes pieced together a play for a publisher, sometimes a company in need of money sold a play, and sometimes a company allowed a play to be published that no longer drew audiences. That Shakespeare did not concern himself with publication, then, is scarcely remarkable; of his contemporaries only Ben Jonson carefully supervised the publication of his own plays. In 1623, seven years after Shakespeare's death, John Heminges and Henry Condell (two senior members of Shakespeare's company, who had performed with him for about twenty years) collected his plays—published and unpublished—into a large volume, commonly called the First Folio. (A folio is a volume consisting of sheets that have been folded once, each sheet thus making two leaves, or four pages. The eighteen plays published during Shakespeare's lifetime had been issued one play per volume in small books called quartos. Each sheet in a quarto has been folded twice, making four leaves, or eight pages.) The First Folio contains thirty-six plays; a thirty-seventh, *Pericles,* though not in the Folio, is regarded as canonical. Heminges and Condell suggest in an address "To the great variety of readers" that the republished plays are presented in better form than in the quartos: "Before you were abused with diverse stolen and surreptitious copies, maimed and deformed by the frauds and stealths of injurious impostors that exposed them; even those, are now offered to your view cured and perfect of their limbs, and all the rest absolute in their numbers, as he [i.e., Shakespeare] conceived them."

Whoever was assigned to prepare the texts for publication in the First Folio seems to have taken his job seriously and yet not to have performed it with uniform care. The sources of the texts seem to have been, in general, good unpublished copies or the best published copies.

The first play in the collection, *The Tempest,* is divided into acts and scenes, has unusually full stage directions and descriptions of spectacle, and concludes with a list of the characters, but the editor was not able (or willing) to present all of the succeeding texts so fully dressed. Later texts occasionally show signs of carelessness: in one scene of *Much Ado About Nothing* the names of actors, instead of characters, appear as speech prefixes, as they had in the quarto, which the Folio reprints; proofreading throughout the Folio is spotty and apparently was done without reference to the printer's copy; the pagination of *Hamlet* jumps from 156 to 257.

A modern editor of Shakespeare must first select his copy; no problem if the play exists only in the Folio, but a considerable problem if the relationship between a quarto and the Folio—or an early quarto and a later one —is unclear. When an editor has chosen what seems to him to be the most authoritative text or texts for his copy, he has not done with making decisions. First of all, he must reckon with Elizabethan spelling. If he is not producing a facsimile, he probably modernizes it, but ought he to preserve the old form of words that apparently were pronounced quite unlike their modern forms—"lanthorn" "alablaster"? If he preserves these forms, is he really preserving Shakespeare's forms or perhaps those of a compositor in the printing house? What is one to do when one finds "lanthorn" and "lantern" in adjacent lines? (The editors of this series in general, but not invariably, assume that words should be spelled in their modern form.) Elizabethan punctuation, too, presents problems. For example in the First Folio, the only text for the play, Macbeth rejects his wife's idea that he can wash the blood from his hand:

> no: this my Hand will rather
> The multitudinous Seas incarnardine,
> Making the Greene one, Red.

Obviously an editor will remove the superfluous capitals, and he will probably alter the spelling to "incarnadine," but will he leave the comma before "red," letting Macbeth speak of the sea as "the green one," or will he (like most modern editors) remove the comma and thus have Macbeth say that his hand will make the ocean *uniformly* red?

An editor will sometimes have to change more than spelling or punctuation. Macbeth says to his wife:

> I dare do all that may become a man,
> Who dares no more, is none.

For two centuries editors have agreed that the second line is unsatisfactory, and have emended "no" to "do": "Who dares do more is none." But when in the same play Ross says that fearful persons

> floate vpon a wilde and violent Sea
> Each way, and moue,

need "move" be emended to "none," as it often is, on the hunch that the compositor misread the manuscript? The editors of the Signet Classic Shakespeare have restrained themselves from making abundant emendations. In their minds they hear Dr. Johnson on the dangers of emending: "I have adopted the Roman sentiment, that it is more honorable to save a citizen than to kill an enemy." Some departures (in addition to spelling, punctuation, and lineation) from the copy text have of course been made, but the original readings are listed in a note following the play, so that the reader can evaluate them for himself.

The editors of the Signet Classic Shakespeare, following tradition, have added line numbers and in many cases act and scene divisions as well as indications of locale at the beginning of scenes. The Folio divided most of the plays into acts and some into scenes. Early eighteenth-century editors increased the divisions. These divisions, which provide a convenient way of referring to passages in the plays, have been retained, but when not in the text chosen as the basis for the Signet Classic text they are enclosed in square brackets [ ] to indicate that they are editorial additions. Similarly, although no play of Shakespeare's published during his lifetime was equipped with indications of locale at the heads of scene divisions, locales have here been added in square brackets for the convenience of the reader, who lacks the information afforded to spectators by costumes, properties, and gestures. The spectator can tell at a glance he is in the throne room, but without an editorial indication the reader may be puzzled for a while. It should be mentioned, incidentally, that there are a few authentic stage directions—perhaps Shakespeare's, perhaps a prompter's—that suggest locales: for example, "Enter Brutus in his orchard," and "They go up into the Senate house." It is hoped that the bracketed additions provide the reader with the sort of help provided in these two authentic directions, but it is equally hoped that the reader will remember that the stage was not loaded with scenery.

No editor during the course of his work can fail to recollect some words Heminges and Condell prefixed to the Folio:

> It had been a thing, we confess, worthy to have been wished, that the author himself had lived to have set forth and overseen his own writings. But since it hath been ordained otherwise, and he by death departed from that right, we pray you do not envy his friends the office of their care and pain to have collected and published them.

Nor can an editor, after he has done his best, forget Heminges and Condell's final words: "And so we leave you to other of his friends, whom if you need can be your guides. If you need them not, you can lead yourselves, and others. And such readers we wish him."

SYLVAN BARNET
Tufts University

Introduction

The Tempest is probably the last play wholly written by Shakespeare. Generations of readers have for this reason been tempted to see it as a culmination of Shakespeare's vision, to identify Prospero with Shakespeare, and to read the famous speech in which Prospero breaks his magic wand as Shakespeare's farewell to his art. Although critics nowadays hesitate to identify Prospero with Shakespeare, those of us who love *The Tempest* cannot help feeling that it represents a culmination—that Shakespeare could not have written it without the wisdom and technique he had accumulated through writing all his other plays.

We get this impression because the characterizations, for example, are so simple—Prospero is wise, Miranda is pure, Caliban is base, Antonio is wicked. Yet these are not the simple characters of a playwright who cannot do any better. They are the simple characters of the playwright who has already created Hamlet and Macbeth and Lear. And we feel this; we feel we are in touch, through the characters of *The Tempest,* with very real and very powerful forces. Caliban, who speaks one of the most beautiful passages of poetry in the play, is enigmatic enough. But where will you come to an end of understanding Ariel? Ariel's complexity certainly does not lie in his characterization. It lies, you may say, in the poetry he speaks. But that is to beg the question.

It is the deliberate return to naïveté, after the tragic complexity, that makes us feel there is something special about the four plays of Shakespeare's final period. The special effect is most apparent in *The Tempest,* because it is the lightest in surface of the four. It is presented to us as a gorgeous bubble, which is blown up for our entertainment like the masque Prospero conjures for Ferdinand and Miranda, and which is just as easily dispelled in the end. Yet *The Tempest* contains the subject matter of tragedy, and it gives us throughout the sense of omniscience, of surveying all life, that we get only at the highest points of illumination in the tragedies. No wonder then that *The Tempest* seems the appropriate statement of age, of the man who having seen it all can teach us that the profoundest statement is the lightest and that life, when we see through it, is gay, is tragicomically gay —that the evil, the violence, the tragedy are all part of a providential design.

The Tempest was probably written during the fall and winter of 1610–1611. It was produced at court in the fall of 1611, and again during the winter of 1612–1613 as part of the festivities that preceded the marriage of the King's daughter Elizabeth to the Elector Palatine. The First Folio probably gives us the play as it was acted at court during the winter. But there is insufficient evidence to support the contention of some scholars that the play was radically revised for the wedding festivities and that the wedding masque in Act IV was inserted in honor of the betrothed couple. Some scholars have even, in their disappointment with the verse of the wedding masque, supposed that the masque was not written by Shakespeare. But Shakespeare always uses a deliberately stilted style for a play within a play; and the masque depends for its effectiveness on spectacle rather than language. Unless new external evidence turns up, there is no reason to look outside the play itself for an explanation of the wedding masque, since the masque fits in subject matter and form into the very texture of *The Tempest*.

The masque brings to a climax the theme of nature versus art that is central to *The Tempest*. For Heaven and Earth, Juno and Ceres, unite in the masque to pronounce a blessing on the union of Ferdinand and Miranda, and to connect sexual union with nature's fruitfulness as seen in its ideal aspect. Venus and her son Cupid are, however, as representatives of lawless passion, specifically excluded from the natural force celebrated in the masque. This fits in with Prospero's severe warning to Ferdinand not to "break" Miranda's "virgin knot" before marriage. Nature is celebrated in the masque as a principle of order. And it is shown to be, as a principle of order, inextricably intertwined with art, civilization, idea.

There is good reason to believe that Shakespeare had in mind, when he wrote *The Tempest,* the reports that first reached England in September 1610 of the miraculous deliverance of the crew and passengers of a ship that had been lost the year before in a terrible tempest off the Bermudas—those stormy islands that Shakespeare refers to in *The Tempest* as "the still-vexed Bermoothes." The written accounts of the survivors (extracts from which appear under "The Source of *The Tempest*") emphasize the providential quality of their deliverance, for the castaways were saved by the magically beneficent nature of the island on which they found themselves. These so-called Bermuda pamphlets go on to see the very storm and shipwreck as providential, since they enabled the castaways to discover for the benefit of mankind that the islands that mariners had shunned as inhabited by devils were actually an island paradise.

In exclaiming over the ways of providence, the Bermuda pamphlets offer those paradoxes that are at the heart of the tragicomic vision—the sort of paradoxes Shakespeare uses in *The Tempest*. "Though the seas threaten, they are merciful," says Ferdinand in the end. And Gonzalo sums up the meaning of the play through a series of paradoxes. "Was Milan thrust from Milan, that his issue/ Should become kings of Naples?" he asks.

> In one voyage
> Did Claribel her husband find at Tunis,
> And Ferdinand her brother found a wife
> Where he himself was lost; Prospero his dukedom
> In a poor isle; and all of us ourselves
> When no man was his own.

(V.i.208–13)

This is the essential message of tragicomedy—that we lose in order to recover something greater, that we die in order to be reborn to a better life. One of the Bermuda pamphlets speaks paradoxically of "these infortunate (yet fortunate) islands," and even calls the shipwreck and deliverance "this tragical comedy."

The Bermuda episode must have raised again for Shakespeare the perennial question that became particularly pertinent after the discovery of the New World—the question of whether nature is not superior to art, and whether man is not nobler in a state of nature than in a state of civilization. It is not surprising that Shakespeare had also in mind, when he wrote *The Tempest,* the essay "Of the Cannibals" (also extracted under "Source") in which Montaigne praises the American Indians in terms that helped establish the ideal of the Noble Savage. Gonzalo's description of his ideal commonwealth is a close paraphrase of Montaigne's essay.

The island of *The Tempest* is in the Mediterranean, somewhere between Tunis and Naples; yet it seems more magically remote and unlocated than if it had been given a specific location, even one so far as the Bermudas. By setting his island in the Mediterranean, Shakespeare is able to bring the European tradition to bear on the question of nature versus art. He can assimilate the latest ideas about the New World to traditional ideas of the Golden Age and the Garden of Eden. He can remind us of Aeneas, who lost Troy that he might found Rome. Aeneas was driven by a storm to Carthage (specifically associated here with Tunis), from whence he sailed to Italy. In fulfilling his destiny, he underwent wanderings and ordeals analogous to those of the court party in *The Tempest,* including a banquet involving harpies. It is worth mentioning, in connection with Gonzalo's enigmatic references to "widow Dido" and "widower Aeneas," that two of the Bermuda pamphlets compare Dido and Aeneas, as colonizers of new territories, to the colonists of the New World.

Shakespeare addresses himself to the question of nature versus art by ringing all possible changes on the meaning of "nature." Caliban is natural in that he is earthy and earthbound, low, material. But Ariel is just as natural in that he represents the fluid elements of water and air and also those bodiless energies of nature that strike us as "spiritual." Caliban, whose name may derive from "cannibal," is the natural man seen in one aspect. But Miranda is also natural, and the two are contrasted throughout. Both were brought up in a state of nature; and if Miranda never saw a man other than her father, Caliban never saw a woman other than his mother. Caliban is natural in the sense that nature is rudimentary and mindless; he cannot be educated. Miranda is natural in the sense that we take the Golden Age or the Garden of Eden to be our natural condition. She has been superbly educated by Prospero, but education has with her been absorbed in the natural; knowledge has not lost her the Garden.

The case of Caliban is complex, because we cannot be certain that he is human. He was begotten by a devil on the witch Sycorax, and he is spoken of either as something between an animal and a man, or as something between a sea and a land animal. All the ironic changes on the meaning of "nature" can be heard in Trinculo's remark about Caliban: "That a monster should be such a natural!"—in which "natural" means "idiot." If we take nature to be a principle of order, then the primitive Caliban is a monster, a piece of disorder or deformity.

Trinculo's remark contrasts with Miranda's, when she thinks Ferdinand must be a god, "for nothing natural/ I ever saw so noble." Ferdinand, too, and in the end Alonso think for the same reason that Miranda must be a goddess. Shakespeare would seem to be telling us that your view of the natural depends on your view of the supernatural— on whether you see behind natural phenomena the evil machinations of the witch Sycorax and her devil-god Setebos, or whether you see at work a rational and benevolent providence. He seems to be telling us that every creature can be judged by its potential metamorphoses, by what it is capable of becoming. Miranda sees all the human beings in the play as godlike. But Caliban, who constantly shifts before our eyes between human and animal, fears that he and his drunken co-conspirators will turn into apes or into barnacles, geese believed to be the product of metamorphosis from shellfish.

There is no question as to which view of nature Shakespeare adheres to. He presents here, as in the history plays and the tragedies, a grand vision of order in nature and society; only the emphasis here, far more than in his other plays, is on nature. The fact that Caliban takes the drunken butler, Stephano, for a god is a sign of how high man ranks on the scale of life. It is because we recognize the differences of degree within the human scale that we laugh at Caliban's illusion, but give our poetic faith to the illusion of Ferdinand and Miranda when they take each other for divine. Caliban's crime in conspiring against Prospero is a sin against degree—like the plot of Antonio and Sebastian against Alonso, and Antonio's usurpation of Prospero's throne. Prospero erred in attempting to educate Caliban, just as he erred in allowing Antonio to play the duke in Milan. In both cases, he blurred distinctions of degree and helped create the disorder that followed.

Caliban is only evil when judged by human standards, or when he himself aspires to get above his place. In attempting to be "free," he only exchanges masters; for a slave he is and should be, as he himself recognizes in the end. Ariel, on the other hand, is by nature a free spirit (he seems free enough even in the bondage of which he complains), and he is therefore appropriately freed in the end. There is a connection in Shakespeare's worldview between biological and social rank and moral obligation. Thus, Antonio's crime against his brother and sovereign is also spoken of as "unnatural." But Antonio is much worse than Caliban, because much higher up on the scale. For the same reason, Stephano and Trinculo seem even baser than Caliban and even more ridiculous in their aspiration to get above themselves.

With the exception of Antonio, all the characters in the play are saved in the end according to their degree. They undergo a ritual temptation and punishment. Caliban, Stephano, and Trinculo are befouled in a horse-pond for their temptation to murder Prospero; and when Stephano and Trinculo are tempted to steal the clothes left out for them as bait, all three conspirators are chased away by spirits in the shape of dogs. These punishments are appropriate to the level of their moral life.

The court party are ritualistically tempted and punished by the banquet that disappears when they start to eat of it. Antonio and Sebastian have also been tempted to murder Alonso; and Alonso has been ritualistically punished by the supposed loss of his son and by his brother's temptation to do to him what he helped Antonio do to Prospero. When Ariel, who is invisible to everyone except Prospero, accuses Alonso, Antonio, and Sebastian of being "three men of sin," his voice comes to them as an inner voice. Alonso's attack of conscience comes as a total illumination. He now understands the union of the natural and moral order:

> Methought the billows spoke and told me of it;
> The winds did sing it to me; and the thunder,
> . . . .
>   did bass my trespass.
> Therefore my son i' th' ooze is bedded.
>   (III.iii.96–100)

Since Ferdinand and Miranda start without guilt, their development is mystical rather than moral. Ferdinand's ordeal prepares him to share with Miranda the vision of heaven on earth that Prospero sets before them in the wedding masque. They themselves appear in a masque-like vision of perfection, when Prospero draws a curtain to reveal them to the court party. Note that Ferdinand repeats in his ordeal the bondage of Caliban. But bondage at the lovers' high level of existence is transformed into freedom and happiness.

Prospero himself is, I think, tempted, when he remembers Caliban's conspiracy against him, to take revenge against the court party; for Caliban's conspiracy reminds him of the conspiracy of Antonio and Alonso. It is inconsistent with Prospero's role of a providence in the play to suppose that he did not from the start plan for events to work out as they do, and that he is actually converted from some original purpose of revenge by Ariel's remark that he would pity the court party were he human. Since Prospero obviously planned the marriage of Ferdinand and Miranda, it is likely that he also planned to be reconciled with Alonso and the others and that Ariel recalls him to his purpose. The point where, at the thought of Caliban, Prospero interrupts the masque, and is shaken by emotion, is the one point where he seems fallible like the other human beings in the play. We seem to be getting, in his lapse from and return to his purpose, the repetition of a moral conversion from thoughts of revenge that took place before the play begins. All the tragic events of Prospero's earlier life are portrayed for us through such repetitions; so that the tragic events appear to us in a comic perspective, since we now see how well everything turned out.

Almost all the characters pair off. As sovereign and father, Prospero pairs off with Alonso; and as magician, he pairs off with Caliban's mother, the witch Sycorax, who practiced black magic on the island as against Prospero's white magic. Ferdinand pairs off with Miranda; Antonio with Sebastian; Stephano with Trinculo; Caliban with Ariel. In his role of providence, Prospero stands alone at the top of the design. Such symmetries are at the heart of comic technique, perhaps because they make us feel we are seeing events from above, as part of a pattern, and can therefore restrain sympathy in the confidence that all is well. The design also explains the sense in which Shakespeare is not realistic in *The Tempest*. He is dealing in simplifications like those of the mathematician. He is giving us a diagram of the order of things.

The play begins with a scene of disorder—a tempest at sea that renders meaningless the usual social order. The sailors are disrespectful to the aristocrats, who in trying to assert authority get in the way of the ship's organization. The good-humored courage of Gonzalo stands out against the irrationality of Antonio and Sebastian, who scream abuse at the sailors—though they are later in the play to think themselves very rational in plotting social disorder. The storm gives the boatswain a chance to display a natural superiority that has nothing to do with rank.

In the next scene, we learn that the tempest is an illusion created to regenerate the social order—to restore a reformed Prospero to the throne of Milan, and to lead Ferdinand and Miranda to the throne of Naples. Ariel turns the noise and confusion of the tempest into music, the music that leads Ferdinand to Miranda. The play is pervaded, as G. Wilson Knight has shown in *The Shakespearean Tempest,* by the imagery of tempest, sea, natural noise, and music. This imagery sets the play in a world where disorder is seen to be not merely at the service of order, but inextricably intertwined, indeed identical, with it. It requires only a transformation of perception to recognize order in disorder.

It is, I think, because Ariel makes music out of the natural noises of the island that there is an undersong of animal noises behind one of his songs, and the sound of the sea behind another. When Caliban says, "Be not afeard; the isle is full of noises,/ Sounds and sweet airs that give delight and hurt not," he catches the world of nature between metamorphoses, between noise and music, sleep and waking. We say he renders the magical atmosphere of the island. We mean by this that, like Ariel in his songs, Caliban in this lovely speech shows the appearances of things as fluid and ever-changing aspects of a single force—a force that is beneficent, though it may seem in certain aspects evil.

This force is represented by the sea that washes through every nook and cranny of the play, moving the characters to their destiny both by carrying them there and by washing right up into their consciousness. When Prospero tells Miranda of the "sea sorrow" that brought them to the island, he describes the sea as both threatening and loving. We were cast adrift, he says,

> To cry to th' sea that roared to us; to sigh
> To th' winds, whose pity, sighing back again,
> Did us but loving wrong.
>
> (I.ii.149–51)

The supposed drowning of Ferdinand is spoken of in attractive images. And when one of Alonso's courtiers suggests that Ferdinand may have made it to land, he makes us see that, by struggling against the waves, Ferdinand actually rode them to shore as you ride a fiery steed.

> I saw him beat the surges under him
> And ride upon their backs. He trod the water,
> Whose enmity he flung aside, and breasted
> The surge most swol'n that met him. His bold head
> 'Bove the contentious waves he kept, and oared
> Himself with his good arms in lusty stroke
> To th' shore . . .
>
> (II.i.119–25)

The passage—which is, in its complexity of implication and its metrical suppleness, a good example of Shakespeare's late style—turns violence into harmony. It is but a step away from the song in which Ariel makes drowning seem so desirable, because it is, like all aspects of existence in this play, "a sea change/ Into something rich and strange" —into the one force that moves all things. Prospero's magic is a portion of nature's; his providential design is a portion of God's.

Antonio, when he tempts Sebastian to murder the King, uses sea imagery, connecting it with the imagery of sleep and dream to signify the force of Sebastian's real desire. Antonio speaks, through his imagery, truer than he knows; for even his plot is necessary to the providential design of the play. Antonio is an effective villain, because he manipulates real, which is to say magical, forces. Prospero uses the imagery of metamorphosis when he tells Miranda how Antonio so transformed the Milanese court as to make real Antonio's appearance of being duke. The wild sounds of sea and tempest turn for Alonso into rational music that tells him of his crime. And Prospero brings the sea imagery to a climax when he says in the end of the court party,

> Their understanding
> Begins to swell, and the approaching tide
> Will shortly fill the reasonable shore,
> That now lies foul and muddy.
> (V.i.79–82)

The sea is now identified with rationality.

The most admirable characters are those who can perceive order in disorder, because they have the capacity for wonder. When Ferdinand says "Admired Miranda," he is playing on the meaning of her name; he is saying, "O wonderful woman, who is to be wondered at." And when, during the masque, he calls Prospero "So rare a wond'red father" (a father possessed of wonders and therefore to be wondered at), it is a sign that he now sees Prospero right. There is an irony in Miranda's famous remark at the end, when she first beholds the court party:

> O, wonder!
> How many goodly creatures are there here!
> How beauteous mankind is! O brave new world
> That has such people in't!
> (V.i.181–84)

Nevertheless, it is the whole point of the play to make us feel that Miranda is right—that she, in her innocence, sees all these people as they really are, as through all their metamorphoses they are tending to be.

It is to Caliban's credit that he exhibits a capacity for wonder lacking in Stephano and Trinculo and in Antonio and Sebastian. That is because Caliban is natural. His faults do not stem from a perversion of reason, as do those of the four witty characters who do not exhibit a capacity for wonder. Only Gonzalo combines both wit and wonder. In the first appearance of the court party, we see how differently the same phenomena may strike different people. For only Gonzalo sees that their deliver-

ance was miraculous and that the island is a paradise. To
be in the Garden of Eden is, we are to understand, a
matter of perception. Antonio and Sebastian are with their
witty quibbling—their quibble, for example, over the few
miles that separate modern Tunis from ancient Carthage
—merely destructive.

The effect of wonder is created in *The Tempest* through
a combination of several genres—tragicomedy, pastoral,
romance, and masque. Antonio's temptation of Sebastian
has been compared to the temptation of Macbeth by Lady
Macbeth; it is the stuff of tragedy. Our view of it, however, is comic, because we know that Ariel is watching
over the scene and has brought it about as part of Prospero's design. The whole action is comic in this sense.
The abbreviation of time (*The Tempest* and *The Comedy
of Errors* are the only plays in which Shakespeare ob-
serves the classical unity of time) enables us to see even
Prospero's tragedy in Milan as, in retrospect, for the
best. The comic perspective does not, however, make us
laugh. It makes us marvel.

Not only the tragedy, but the comedy, too, is dissolved
in wonder. Bernard Knox has, in the essay reprinted in
this volume, connected *The Tempest* with Roman comedies about slaves. Nevertheless, Caliban and Ariel are
too marvelous to be laughed at as we laugh at the slaves
in Roman comedies. Stephano and Trinculo seem a kind
of comic relief, just because we do so little laughing at
the main action of *The Tempest*. Through Prospero's eyes,
The Tempest shows us life as God must see it. God could
not view life tragically, because He knows that all is for
the best. God also knows, as Prospero knows of Ferdinand, that the ordeals He sets for us are for our own good
and are not so hard or serious as we think them. Neither,
however, could God laugh at us as we laugh at the characters in comedies; for He would not ridicule us, or be
dazzled by our wit.

Prospero's view of life is set forth in the famous speech
in which he says, after dispelling the wedding masque,
"We are such stuff/ As dreams are made on." He is, I
think, recovering his perspective in this speech after the

relapse into thoughts of revenge. The speech is, like Miranda's exclamations, an expression of the marvelous quality of life. Prospero implies, in consoling Ferdinand for the disappearance of the masque, that if life is as illusory as the masque, it is also as gorgeously illusory. He implies also that there is a reality behind life just as there is Prospero behind the masque.

In his detachment from the appearances of life, Prospero regains an innocence of vision analogous to Miranda's. It is the vision of pastoral, the genre that deals with man and nature in their unfallen state. By swiftly recapitulating all the facts of life, tragicomedy leads us to see through life with the eyes of Miranda who never left the Garden. Tragicomedy uses to this end the devices of romance. For romance deals in marvelous events and solves its problems through metamorphoses and recognition scenes—through, in other words, transformations of perception. When Alonso recognizes Prospero and Ferdinand, both of whom he had thought dead, he recognizes their magical preciousness and thus really *sees* them for the first time. The same is true of the crew's response to the ship, when it is magically restored to them. The recognized objects are transformed through the transformed eyes of the beholders; so that more is restored than has been lost.

The masque, with its emphasis on spectacle and surprise, subordinates all other effects to the effect of wonder. "The fringed curtains of thine eye advance," says Prospero to Miranda when the spectacle of Ferdinand is about to break upon her. It is as though a theater curtain were to be raised; as, indeed, it is raised or drawn when the spectacle of the lovers breaks upon the court party. All the scenes that offer the characters illumination are masquelike and illusory. Yet it is through these illusions that the characters come to understand reality. We all found ourselves, says Gonzalo in the end, "when no man was his own."

Art is just such an experience of enchantment. The speech in which Prospero breaks his magic wand is not so much Shakespeare's farewell to his art as it is his comment on the relation between art and life. For in breaking his wand and taking himself and the others back to Italy, Prospero seems to be saying that the enchanted island is no abiding place, but rather a place through which we pass in order to renew and strengthen our sense of reality.

In spite of its fantastic elements, *The Tempest,* as F. R. Leavis has pointed out, never confuses but rather clarifies our sense of reality. That is no small part of its achievement—though it is characteristic of our time that Leavis prefers *The Winter's Tale* just because it is less realistic than *The Tempest*. With its bias against realism, and its interest in a symbolic art, our time is better equipped than any time since Shakespeare's to appreciate the last plays. The seventeenth and eighteenth centuries liked best of all Shakespeare's early comedies. The nineteenth century liked the tragedies best, and on the whole we still do. But it may be that the last plays—and especially *The Tempest,* which is as I see it the best of them—will in future have most to say to us. Certainly, the interest in them has in the last generation risen steadily.

ROBERT LANGBAUM
University of Virginia

The Tempest

The Scene: An uninhabited island.

Names of the Actors

Alonso, King of Naples
Sebastian, his brother
Prospero, the right Duke of Milan
Antonio, his brother, the usurping Duke of Milan
Ferdinand, son to the King of Naples
Gonzalo, an honest old councilor
Adrian and Francisco, lords
Caliban, a savage and deformed slave
Trinculo, a jester
Stephano, a drunken butler
Master of a ship
Boatswain
Mariners
Miranda, daughter to Prospero
Ariel, an airy spirit
Iris
Ceres
Juno } [presented by] spirits
Nymphs
Reapers
[Other Spirits attending on Prospero]

The Tempest

ACT I

Scene I. [*On a ship at sea.*]

A tempestuous noise of thunder and lightning heard. Enter a Shipmaster and a Boatswain.

Master. Boatswain!

Boatswain. Here, master. What cheer?

Master. Good,°¹ speak to th' mariners! Fall to't yarely,° or we run ourselves aground. Bestir, bestir!
                                                    Exit.

                    Enter Mariners.

Boatswain. Heigh, my hearts! Cheerly, cheerly, my   5
hearts! Yare, yare! Take in the topsail! Tend to th'
master's whistle! Blow till thou burst thy wind, if
room enough!°

Enter Alonso, Sebastian, Antonio, Ferdinand, Gonzalo, and others.

Alonso. Good boatswain, have care. Where's the
master? Play the men.°   10

Boatswain. I pray now, keep below.

¹ The degree sign (°) indicates a footnote, which is keyed to the
text by line number. Text references are printed in *italic* type; the
annotation follows in roman type.
I.i.3. *Good* good fellow   4 *yarely* briskly   7–8 *Blow till . . . room
enough* the storm can blow and split itself as long as there is open
sea without rocks to maneuver in   10 *Play the men* act like men

Antonio. Where is the master, bos'n?

Boatswain. Do you not hear him? You mar our labor.
    Keep your cabins; you do assist the storm.

15 *Gonzalo.* Nay, good, be patient.

Boatswain. When the sea is. Hence! What cares these
    roarers for the name of king? To cabin! Silence!
    Trouble us not!

Gonzalo. Good, yet remember whom thou hast
20   aboard.

Boatswain. None that I more love than myself. You
    are a councilor; if you can command these elements
    to silence and work the peace of the present,° we
    will not hand° a rope more. Use your authority.
25   If you cannot, give thanks you have lived so long,
    and make yourself ready in your cabin for the mis-
    chance of the hour, if it so hap. Cheerly, good
    hearts! Out of our way, I say.   *Exit.*

Gonzalo. I have great comfort from this fellow. Me-
30   thinks he hath no drowning mark upon him; his
    complexion is perfect gallows.° Stand fast, good
    Fate, to his hanging! Make the rope of his destiny
    our cable, for our own doth little advantage.° If he
    be not born to be hanged, our case is miserable.
                                Exit [with the rest].

Enter Boatswain.

35 *Boatswain.* Down with the topmast! Yare! Lower,
    lower! Bring her to try with main course!° (*A cry
    within.*) A plague upon this howling! They are
    louder than the weather or our office.°

---

23 *work the peace of the present* restore the present to peace (since
as a councilor his job is to quell disorder)   24 *hand* handle   30-
31 *no drowning mark . . . gallows* (alluding to the proverb, "He
that's born to be hanged need fear no drowning")   33 *doth little advantage* gives us little advantage   36 *Bring her to try with main
course* heave to, under the mainsail   37-38 *They are louder . . .
office* these passengers make more noise than the tempest or than we
do at our work

Enter Sebastian, Antonio, and Gonzalo.

Yet again? What do you here? Shall we give o'er°
and drown? Have you a mind to sink?   40

Sebastian. A pox o' your throat, you bawling, blas-
phemous, incharitable dog!

Boatswain. Work you, then.

Antonio. Hang, cur! Hang, you whoreson, insolent
noisemaker! We are less afraid to be drowned than   45
thou art.

Gonzalo. I'll warrant him for° drowning, though the
ship were no stronger than a nutshell and as leaky
as an unstanched° wench.

Boatswain. Lay her ahold, ahold! Set her two   50
courses!° Off to sea again! Lay her off!°

Enter Mariners wet.

Mariners. All lost! To prayers, to prayers! All lost!
                                          [*Exeunt.*]

Boatswain. What, must our mouths be cold?

Gonzalo. The King and Prince at prayers! Let's assist
them,
For our case is as theirs.

Sebastian.   I am out of patience.   55

Antonio. We are merely° cheated of our lives by
drunkards.
This wide-chopped° rascal—would thou mightst lie
drowning
The washing of ten tides!°

---

39 *give o'er* give up trying to run the ship   47 *warrant him for*
guarantee him against   49 *unstanched* wide-open   50–51 *Lay her
ahold. . . . courses* (the ship is still being blown dangerously to shore,
so the boatswain orders that the foresail be set in addition to the
mainsail; but the ship still moves toward shore)   51 *Lay her off* i.e.,
away from the shore   56 *merely* completely   57 *wide-chopped* big-
mouthed   58 *ten tides* (pirates were hanged on the shore and left
there until three tides had washed over them)

Gonzalo.   He'll be hanged yet,
  Though every drop of water swear against it
  And gape at wid'st to glut him.

60   *A confused noise within:* "Mercy on us!"
  "We split, we split!" "Farewell, my wife and chil-
      dren!"
  "Farewell, brother!" "We split, we split, we split!"
                                [*Exit Boatswain.*]

Antonio. Let's all sink wi' th' King.

Sebastian.   Let's take leave of him.
                                Exit [*with Antonio*].

Gonzalo. Now would I give a thousand furlongs of
65   sea for an acre of barren ground—long heath,°
  brown furze, anything. The wills above be done,
  but I would fain die a dry death.   *Exit.*

Scene II. [*The island. In front of Prospero's cell.*]

Enter Prospero and Miranda.

Miranda. If by your art, my dearest father, you have
  Put the wild waters in this roar, allay them.
  The sky, it seems, would pour down stinking pitch
  But that the sea, mounting to th' welkin's cheek,°
5 Dashes the fire out. O, I have suffered
  With those that I saw suffer! A brave° vessel
  (Who had no doubt some noble creature in her)
  Dashed all to pieces! O, the cry did knock

---

65 *heath* heather   I.ii.4 *welkin's cheek* face of the sky   6 *brave* fine,
gallant (the word often has this meaning in the play)

Against my very heart! Poor souls, they perished!
Had I been any god of power, I would   10
Have sunk the sea within the earth or ere
It should the good ship so have swallowed and
The fraughting° souls within her.

Prospero.   Be collected.
No more amazement.° Tell your piteous heart
There's no harm done.

Miranda.   O, woe the day!

Prospero.   No harm.   15
I have done nothing but in care of thee,
Of thee my dear one, thee my daughter, who
Art ignorant of what thou art, naught knowing
Of whence I am, nor that I am more better
Than Prospero, master of a full poor cell,   20
And thy no greater father.°

Miranda.   More to know
Did never meddle° with my thoughts.

Prospero.   'Tis time
I should inform thee farther. Lend thy hand
And pluck my magic garment from me. So.
                          [*Lays down his robe.*]
Lie there, my art. Wipe thou thine eyes; have
    comfort.   25
The direful spectacle of the wrack, which touched
The very virtue° of compassion in thee,
I have with such provision° in mine art
So safely ordered that there is no soul—
No, not so much perdition° as an hair   30
Betid° to any creature in the vessel
Which thou heard'st cry, which thou saw'st sink.
    Sit down;
For thou must now know farther.

13 *fraughting* forming her freight   14 *amazement* consternation
21 *thy no greater father* i.e., thy father, no greater than the Prospero
just described   22 *meddle* mingle   27 *virtue* essence   28 *provision*
foresight   30 *perdition* loss   31 *Betid* happened

Miranda.   You have often
　Begun to tell me what I am; but stopped
35　And left me to a bootless inquisition,
　Concluding, "Stay; not yet."

Prospero.   The hour's now come;
　The very minute bids thee ope thine ear.
　Obey, and be attentive. Canst thou remember
　A time before we came unto this cell?
40　I do not think thou canst, for then thou wast not
　Out° three years old.

Miranda.   Certainly, sir, I can.

Prospero. By what? By any other house or person?
　Of anything the image tell me that
　Hath kept with thy remembrance.

Miranda.   'Tis far off,
45　And rather like a dream than an assurance
　That my remembrance warrants.° Had I not
　Four or five women once that tended me?

Prospero. Thou hadst, and more, Miranda. But how
　　is it
　That this lives in thy mind? What seest thou else
50　In the dark backward and abysm of time?
　If thou rememb'rest aught ere thou cam'st here,
　How thou cam'st here thou mayst.

Miranda.   But that I do not.

Prospero. Twelve year since, Miranda, twelve year
　　since,
　Thy father was the Duke of Milan° and
　A prince of power.

55　*Miranda.*   Sir, are not you my father?

-　*Prospero.* Thy mother was a piece° of virtue, and
　Shé said thou wast my daughter; and thy father
　Was Duke of Milan; and his only heir

41 *Out* fully 46 *remembrance warrants* memory guarantees 54
Milan (pronounced "Mílan") 56 *piece* masterpiece

And princess, no worse issued.°

Miranda.   O the heavens!
What foul play had we that we came from thence?   60
Or blessèd was't we did?

Prospero.   Both, both, my girl!
By foul play, as thou say'st, were we heaved thence,
But blessedly holp° hither.

Miranda.   O, my heart bleeds
To think o' th' teen that I have turned you to,°
Which is from° my remembrance! Please you,
   farther.   65

Prospero. My brother and thy uncle, called
   Antonio—
I pray thee mark me—that a brother should
Be so perfidious!—he whom next thyself
Of all the world I loved, and to him put
The manage of my state,° as at that time   70
Through all the signories° it was the first,
And Prospero the prime duke, being so reputed
In dignity, and for the liberal arts
Without a parallel. Those being all my study,
The government I cast upon my brother   75
And to my state grew stranger, being transported
And rapt in secret studies. Thy false uncle—
Dost thou attend me?

Miranda.   Sir, most heedfully.

Prospero. Being once perfected° how to grant suits,
How to deny them, who t' advance, and who   80
To trash for overtopping,° new-created
The creatures that were mine, I say—or changed
   'em,

59 *no worse issued* of no meaner lineage than he   63 *holp* helped
64 *teen that I have turned you to* sorrow I have caused you to remember   65 *from* out of   70 *manage of my state* management of
my domain   71 *signories* lordships (of Italy)   79 *perfected* grown
skillful   81 *trash for overtopping* (1) check the speed of (as of
hounds) (2) cut down to size (as of overtall trees) the aspirants
for political favor who are growing too bold

Or else new-formed 'em°—having both the key°
Of officer and office, set all hearts i' th' state
85 To what tune pleased his ear, that now he was
The ivy which had hid my princely trunk
And sucked my verdure out on't. Thou attend'st
not?

RICH.
II. → *negligence in garden*

Miranda. O, good sir, I do.

Prospero.   I pray thee mark me.
I thus neglecting worldly ends, all dedicated
90 To closeness° and the bettering of my mind—
With that which, but by being so retired,
O'erprized all popular rate, in my false brother
Awaked an evil nature,° and my trust,
Like a good parent,° did beget of him
95 A falsehood in its contrary as great
As my trust was, which had indeed no limit,
A confidence sans bound. He being thus lorded—
Not only with what my revenue° yielded
But what my power might else exact, like one
100 Who having into truth—by telling of it,°
Made such a sinner of his memory
To° credit his own lie, he did believe
He was indeed the Duke, out o' th' substitution
And executing th' outward face of royalty
With all prerogative.° Hence his ambition
105   growing—
Dost thou hear?

81–83 *new-created/The creatures . . . new-formed 'em* i.e., he re-
created my following—either exchanging my adherents for his
own, or else transforming my adherents into different people
83 *key* (a pun leading to the musical metaphor)   90 *closeness* se-
clusion   91–93 *With that . . . evil nature* i.e., with that dedication
to the mind which, were it not that it kept me from exercising the
duties of my office would surpass in value all ordinary estimate, I
awakened evil in my brother's nature   94 *good parent* (alluding to
the proverb cited by Miranda in line 120)   98 *revenue* (pronounced
"revènue")   99–100 *like one/Who having . . . of it* i.e., like one
who really had these things—by repeatedly saying he had them
(*into* = unto)   102 *To* as to   103–05 *out o' th' substitution . . .
all prerogative* i.e., as a result of his acting as my substitute and performing the outward functions of royalty with all its prerogatives

Miranda.   Your tale, sir, would cure deafness.

Prospero. To have no screen between this part he
     played
   And him he played it for, he needs will be
   Absolute Milan.° Me (poor man) my library
   Was dukedom large enough. Of temporal royalties   110
   He thinks me now incapable; confederates
   (So dry° he was for sway) wi' th' King of Naples
   To give him annual tribute, do him homage,
   Subject his coronet to his crown, and bend
   The dukedom, yet unbowed (alas, poor Milan!),   115
   To most ignoble stooping.

Miranda.   O the heavens!

Prospero. Mark his condition,° and th' event;° then
     tell me
   If this might be a brother.

Miranda.   I should sin
   To think but nobly of my grandmother.
   Good wombs have borne bad sons.

Prospero.   Now the condition.   120
   This King of Naples, being an enemy
   To me inveterate, hearkens my brother's suit;
   Which was, that he, in lieu o' th' premises°
   Of homage and I know not how much tribute,
   Should presently extirpate me and mine   125
   Out of the dukedom and confer fair Milan,
   With all the honors, on my brother. Whereon,
   A treacherous army levied, one midnight
   Fated to th' purpose, did Antonio open
   The gates of Milan; and, i' th' dead of darkness,   130
   The ministers° for th' purpose hurried thence
   Me and thy crying self.

Miranda.   Alack, for pity!

---

109 *Absolute Milan* Duke of Milan in fact   112 *dry* thirsty
117 *condition* terms of his pact with Naples   117 *event* outcome
123 *in lieu o' th' premises* in return for the guarantees   131 *ministers* agents

I, not rememb'ring how I cried out then,
Will cry it o'er again; it is a hint°
That wrings mine eyes to't.

135 *Prospero.*   Hear a little further,
And then I'll bring thee to the present business
Which now's upon's; without the which this story
Were most impertinent.°

Miranda.   Wherefore did they not
That hour destroy us?

Prospero.   Well demanded, wench.
My tale provokes that question. Dear, they durst
140   not,
So dear the love my people bore me; nor set
A mark so bloody on the business; but,
With colors fairer, painted their foul ends.
In few,° they hurried us aboard a bark;
145 Bore us some leagues to sea, where they prepared
A rotten carcass of a butt,° not rigged,
Nor tackle, sail, nor mast; the very rats
Instinctively have quit it. There they hoist us,
To cry to th' sea that roared to us; to sigh
150 To th' winds, whose pity, sighing back again,
Did us but loving wrong.

Miranda.   Alack, what trouble
Was I then to you!

Prospero.   O, a cherubin
Thou wast that did preserve me! Thou didst smile,
Infusèd with a fortitude from heaven,
155 When I have decked° the sea with drops full salt,
Under my burden groaned; which° raised in me
An undergoing stomach,° to bear up
Against what should ensue.
Miranda.   How came we ashore?

---

134 *hint* occasion   138 *impertinent* inappropriate   144 *few* few
words   146 *butt* tub   155 *decked* covered (wept salt tears into the
sea)   156 *which* i.e., Miranda's smile   157 *undergoing stomach*
spirit of endurance

Prospero. By providence divine.
    Some food we had, and some fresh water, that   *160*
    A noble Neapolitan, Gonzalo,
    Out of his charity, who being then appointed
    Master of this design, did give us, with
    Rich garments, linens, stuffs, and necessaries
    Which since have steaded° much. So, of his gentle-
      ness,   *165*
    Knowing I loved my books, he furnished me
    From mine own library with volumes that
    I prize above my dukedom.

Miranda.   Would I might
    But ever see that man!

Prospero.   Now I arise.
    Sit still, and hear the last of our sea sorrow.   *170*
    Here in this island we arrived; and here
    Have I, thy schoolmaster, made thee more profit
    Than other princess' can,° that have more time
    For vainer hours, and tutors not so careful.

Miranda. Heavens thank you for't! And now I pray
    you, sir—   *175*
    For still 'tis beating in my mind—your reason
    For raising this sea storm?

Prospero.   Know thus far forth.
    By accident most strange, bountiful Fortune
    (Now my dear lady)° hath mine enemies
    Brought to this shore; and by my prescience   *180*
    I find my zenith° doth depend upon
    A most auspicious star, whose influence
    If now I court not, but omit,° my fortunes
    Will ever after droop. Here cease more questions.
    Thou art inclined to sleep. 'Tis a good dullness,   *185*
    And give it way. I know thou canst not choose.
                         [*Miranda sleeps.*]

165 *steaded* been of use   173 *princess' can* princesses can have
179 *Now my dear lady* i.e., formerly my foe, now my patroness
181 *zenith* apex of fortune   183 *omit* neglect

Come away,° servant, come! I am ready now.
Approach, my Ariel! Come!

Enter Ariel.

Ariel. All hail, great master! Grave sir, hail! I come
190 To answer thy best pleasure; be't to fly,
To swim, to dive into the fire, to ride
On the curled clouds. To thy strong bidding task°
Ariel and all his quality.°

Prospero.   Hast thou, spirit,
Performed, to point,° the tempest that I bade thee?

195 *Ariel.* To every article.
I boarded the King's ship. Now on the beak,°
Now in the waist,° the deck,° in every cabin,
I flamed amazement.° Sometime I'd divide
And burn in many places; on the topmast,
200 The yards, and boresprit° would I flame distinctly,°
Then meet and join. Jove's lightnings, the precursors
O' th' dreadful thunderclaps, more momentary
And sight-outrunning were not. The fire and cracks
Of sulfurous roaring the most mighty Neptune
205 Seem to besiege, and make his bold waves tremble;
Yea, his dread trident shake.

Prospero.   My brave spirit!
Who was so firm, so constant, that this coil°
Would not infect his reason?

Ariel.   Not a soul
But felt a fever of the mad and played
210 Some tricks of desperation. All but mariners
Plunged in the foaming brine and quit the vessel,
Then all afire with me. The King's son Ferdinand,

---

187 *Come away* i.e., come from where you are; come here   192 *task*
tax to the utmost   193 *quality* cohorts (Ariel is leader of a band of
spirits)   194 *to point* in every detail   196 *beak* prow   197 *waist*
amidships   197 *deck* poop   198 *flamed amazement* struck terror
by appearing as (St. Elmo's) fire   200 *boresprit* bowsprit   200 *dis-*
tinctly in different places   207 *coil* uproar

With hair up-staring° (then like reeds, not hair),
Was the first man that leapt; cried "Hell is empty,
And all the devils are here!"

Prospero.   Why, that's my spirit!   215
But was not this nigh shore?

Ariel.   Close by, my master.

Prospero. But are they, Ariel, safe?

Ariel.   Not a hair perished.
On their sustaining° garments not a blemish,
But fresher than before; and as thou bad'st me,
In troops I have dispersed them 'bout the isle.   220
The King's son have I landed by himself,
Whom I left cooling of the air with sighs
In an odd angle of the isle, and sitting,
His arms in this sad knot.

                    [*Illustrates with a gesture.*]

Prospero.   Of the King's ship,
The mariners, say how thou hast disposed,   225
And all the rest o' th' fleet.

Ariel.   Safely in harbor
Is the King's ship; in the deep nook where once
Thou call'dst me up at midnight to fetch dew
From the still-vexed Bermoothes,° there she's hid;
The mariners all under hatches stowed,   230
Who, with a charm joined to their suff'red° labor,
I have left asleep. And for the rest o' th' fleet,
Which I dispersed, they all have met again,
And are upon the Mediterranean flote°
Bound sadly home for Naples,   '235
Supposing that they saw the King's ship wracked
And his great person perish.

Prospero.   Ariel, thy charge
Exactly is performed; but there's more work.

---

213 *up-staring* standing on end   218 *sustaining* buoying them up
229 *Bermoothes* Bermudas   231 *suff'red* undergone   234 *flote* sea

What is the time o' th' day?

Ariel.   Past the mid season.°

Prospero. At least two glasses.° The time 'twixt six
240   and now
        Must by us both be spent most preciously.

Ariel. Is there more toil? Since thou dost give me
        pains,°
        Let me remember° thee what thou hast promised,
        Which is not yet performed me.

Prospero.   How now? Moody?
        What is't thou canst demand?

245 *Ariel.*   My liberty.

Prospero. Before the time be out? No more!

Ariel.   I prithee,
        Remember I have done thee worthy service,
        Told thee no lies, made thee no mistakings, served
        Without or grudge or grumblings. Thou did
        promise
        To bate me° a full year.

250 *Prospero.* MIND OF PAST ──→ Dost thou forget
        From what a torment I did free thee?

Ariel.   No.

Prospero. Thou dost; and think'st it much to tread
        the ooze
        Of the salt deep,
        To run upon the sharp wind of the North,
255   To do me business in the veins° o' th' earth
        When it is baked° with frost.

Ariel.   I do not, sir.

Prospero. Thou liest, malignant thing! Hast thou
        forgot

239 *mid season* noon   240 *two glasses* two o'clock   242 *pains* hard
tasks   243 *remember* remind   250 *bate me* reduce my term of
service   255 *veins* streams   256 *baked* caked

The foul witch Sycorax,° who with age and envy°
Was grown into a hoop? Hast thou forgot her?

Ariel. No, sir.

Prospero.   Thou hast. Where was she born? Speak!
 Tell me!   260

Ariel. Sir, in Argier.°

Prospero.   O, was she so? I must
 Once in a month recount what thou hast been,
 Which thou forget'st. This damned witch Sycorax,
 For mischiefs manifold, and sorceries terrible
 To enter human hearing, from Argier,   265
 Thou know'st, was banished. For one thing she did
 They would not take her life. Is not this true?

Ariel. Ay, sir.

Prospero. This blue-eyed° hag was hither brought
          with child
 And here was left by th' sailors. Thou, my slave,   270
 As thou report'st thyself, wast then her servant.
 And, for thou wast a spirit too delicate
 To act her earthy and abhorred commands,
 Refusing her grand hests,° she did confine thee,
 By help of her more potent ministers,°   275
 And in her most unmitigable rage,
 Into a cloven pine; within which rift
 Imprisoned thou didst painfully remain
 A dozen years; within which space she died
 And left thee there, where thou didst vent thy
          groans   280
 As fast as millwheels strike. Then was this island
 (Save for the son that she did litter here,
 A freckled whelp, hagborn) not honored with
 A human shape.

258 *Sycorax* (name not found elsewhere; probably derived from
Greek *sys,* "sow," and *korax,* which means both "raven"—see line
322—and "hook"—hence perhaps "hoop") 258 *envy* malice 261
Argier Algiers 269 *blue-eyed* (referring to the livid color of the
eyelid, a sign of pregnancy) 274 *hests* commands 275 *her more
potent ministers* her agents, spirits more powerful than thou

Ariel.   Yes, Caliban her son.

285 *Prospero.* Dull thing, I say so! He, that Caliban
Whom now I keep in service. Thou best know'st
What torment I did find thee in; thy groans
Did make wolves howl and penetrate the breasts
Of ever-angry bears. It was a torment
290 To lay upon the damned, which Sycorax
Could not again undo. It was mine art,
When I arrived and heard thee, that made gape
The pine, and let thee out.

Ariel.   I thank thee, master.

Prospero. If thou more murmur'st, I will rend an oak
295 And peg thee in his° knotty entrails till
Thou hast howled away twelve winters.

Ariel.   Pardon, master.
I will be correspondent° to command
And do my spriting gently.°

Prospero.   Do so; and after two days
I will discharge thee.

Ariel.   That's my noble master!
300 What shall I do? Say what? What shall I do?

Prospero. Go make thyself like a nymph o' th' sea. Be
· subject
To no sight but thine and mine, invisible
To every eyeball else.° Go take this shape
And hither come in't. Go! Hence with diligence!
                     Exit [*Ariel*].
305 Awake, dear heart, awake! Thou hast slept well.
Awake!

Miranda. The strangeness of your story put
Heaviness in me.

---

295 *his* its   **297** *correspondent* obedient   **298** *do my spriting gently*
render graciously my services as a spirit   **302–03** *invisible/To
every eyeball else* (Ariel is invisible to everyone in the play except
Prospero; Henslowe's *Diary*, an Elizabethan stage account, lists
"a robe for to go invisible")

Prospero.   Shake it off. Come on.
We'll visit Caliban, my slave, who never
Yields us kind answer.

Miranda.   'Tis a villain, sir,
I do not love to look on.

Prospero.   But as 'tis,   310
We cannot miss° him. He does make our fire,
Fetch in our wood, and serves in offices
That profit us. What, ho! Slave! Caliban!
Thou earth, thou! Speak!

Caliban. (*Within*)   There's wood enough within.

Prospero. Come forth, I say! There's other business   315
for thee.
Come, thou tortoise! When?°

Enter Ariel like a water nymph.

Fine apparition! My quaint° Ariel,
Hark in thine ear.   [*Whispers.*]

Ariel.   My lord, it shall be done. *Exit.*

Prospero. Thou poisonous slave, got by the devil
himself
Upon thy wicked dam, come forth!   320

Enter Caliban.

Caliban. As wicked dew as e'er my mother brushed
With raven's feather from unwholesome fen
Drop on you both! A southwest blow on ye
And blister you all o'er!

Prospero. For this, be sure, tonight thou shalt have
cramps,   325
Side-stitches that shall pen thy breath up. Urchins°
Shall, for that vast of night that they may work,°

311 *miss* do without   316 *When* (expression of impatience)   317
quaint ingenious   326 *Urchins* goblins in the shape of hedgehogs
327 *vast of night . . . work* (the long, empty stretch of night during
which malignant spirits are allowed to be active)

All exercise on thee; thou shalt be pinched
As thick as honeycomb, each pinch more stinging
Than bees that made 'em.

330   *Caliban.*   I must eat my dinner.
This island's mine by Sycorax my mother,
Which thou tak'st from me. When thou cam'st first,
Thou strok'st me and made much of me; wouldst
    give me
Water with berries in't; and teach me how
335   To name the bigger light, and how the less,
That burn by day and night. And then I loved thee
And showed thee all the qualities o' th' isle,
The fresh springs, brine pits, barren place and
    fertile.
Cursed be I that did so! All the charms
340   Of Sycorax—toads, beetles, bats, light on you!
For I am all the subjects that you have,
Which first was mine own king; and here you sty
    me
In this hard rock, whiles you do keep from me
The rest o' th' island.

Prospero.   Thou most lying slave,
Whom stripes° may move, not kindness! I have
345   used thee
(Filth as thou art) with humane care, and lodged
    thee
In mine own cell till thou didst seek to violate
The honor of my child.

Caliban. O ho, O ho! Would't had been done!
350   Thou didst prevent me; I had peopled else
This isle with Calibans.

Miranda.°   Abhorrèd slave,
Which any print of goodness wilt not take,
Being capable of all ill!° I pitied thee,

DEPENDENCE

---

345 *stripes* lashes   351 (many editors transfer this speech to Prospero as inappropriate to Miranda)   353 *capable of all ill* sus-
ceptible only to evil impressions

Took pains to make thee speak, taught thee each
  hour
One thing or other. When thou didst not, savage,   *355*
Know thine own meaning, but wouldst gabble like
A thing most brutish, I endowed thy purposes
With words that made them known. But thy vile
  race,
Though thou didst learn, had that in't which good
  natures
Could not abide to be with. Therefore wast thou   *360*
Deservedly confined into this rock, who hadst
Deserved more than a prison.

Caliban. You taught me language, and my profit on't
Is, I know how to curse. The red plague rid° you
For learning me your language!

Prospero.   Hagseed, hence!   *365*
Fetch us in fuel. And be quick, thou'rt best,°
To answer other business. Shrug'st thou, malice?
If thou neglect'st or dost unwillingly
What I command, I'll rack thee with old° cramps,
Fill all thy bones with aches,° make thee roar   *370*
That beasts shall tremble at thy din.

Caliban.   No, pray thee.
[*Aside*] I must obey. His art is of such pow'r
It would control my dam's god, Setebos,
And make a vassal of him.

Prospero.   So, slave; hence! *Exit Caliban.*

Enter Ferdinand; and Ariel (*invisible*), *playing
  and singing.*

Ariel's song.

Come unto these yellow sands,   *375*

---

364 *rid* destroy   366 *thou'rt best* you'd better   369 *old* plenty of
(with an additional suggestion, "such as old people have")   370
aches (pronounced "aitches")

And then take hands.
Curtsied when you have and kissed
　The wild waves whist,°
Foot it featly° here and there;
380　And, sweet sprites, the burden bear.
　Hark, hark!
　　　Burden, dispersedly.° Bow, wow!
　The watchdogs bark.
　　　[*Burden, dispersedly.*] Bow, wow!
385　Hark, hark! I hear
　The strain of strutting chanticleer
　　Cry cock-a-diddle-dow.

Ferdinand. Where should this music be? I' th' air or
　　th' earth?
It sounds no more; and sure it waits upon
390　Some god o' th' island. Sitting on a bank,
Weeping again the King my father's wrack,
This music crept by me upon the waters,
Allaying both their fury and my passion°
With its sweet air. Thence I have followed it,
395　Or it hath drawn me rather; but 'tis gone.
No, it begins again.

Ariel's song.

Full fathom five thy father lies;
　Of his bones are coral made;
Those are pearls that were his eyes;
400　　Nothing of him that doth fade
But doth suffer a sea change
Into something rich and strange.
Sea nymphs hourly ring his knell:
　　　Burden. Ding-dong.
405　Hark! Now I hear them—ding-dong bell.

377–78 *kissed/The wild waves whist* i.e., when you have, through
the harmony of kissing in the dance, kissed the wild waves into
silence (?); when you have kissed in the dance, the wild waves being
silenced (?)　379 *featly* nimbly　382 *Burden, dispersedly* (an undersong, coming from all parts of the stage; it imitates the barking
of dogs and perhaps in the end the crowing of a cock)　393 *passion*
grief

Ferdinand. The ditty does remember my drowned
    father.
  This is no mortal business, nor no sound
  That the earth owes.° I hear it now above me.

Prospero. The fringèd curtains of thine eye advance°
  And say what thou seest yond.

Miranda.   What is't? A spirit?   *410*
  Lord, how it looks about! Believe me, sir,
  It carries a brave form. But 'tis a spirit.

Prospero. No, wench; it eats, and sleeps, and hath
    such senses
  As we have, such. This gallant which thou seest
  Was in the wrack; and, but he's something stained   *415*
  With grief (that's beauty's canker), thou mightst
    call him
  A goodly person. He hath lost his fellows
  And strays about to find 'em.

Miranda.   I might call him
  A thing divine; for nothing natural
  I ever saw so noble.

Prospero.   [*Aside*] It goes on, I see,   *420*
  As my soul prompts it. Spirit, fine spirit, I'll free
    thee
  Within two days for this.

Ferdinand.   Most sure, the goddess
  On whom these airs attend! Vouchsafe my prayer
  May know if you remain° upon this island,
  And that you will some good instruction give   *425*
  How I may bear me° here. My prime request,
  Which I do last pronounce, is (O you wonder!)
  If you be maid or no?

Miranda.   No wonder, sir,
  But certainly a maid.

---

408 *owes* owns   409 *advance* raise   423–24 *Vouchsafe my prayer
. . . remain* may my prayer induce you to inform me whether you
dwell   426 *bear me* conduct myself

Ferdinand.   My language? Heavens!
430   I am the best of them that speak this speech,
Were I but where 'tis spoken.

Prospero.   How? The best?
What wert thou if the King of Naples heard thee?

Ferdinand. A single° thing, as I am now, that won-
ders
To hear thee speak of Naples. He does hear me;
435   And that he does I weep. Myself am Naples,
Who with mine eyes, never since at ebb, beheld
The King my father wracked.

Miranda.   Alack, for mercy!

Ferdinand. Yes, faith, and all his lords, the Duke of
Milan
And his brave son° being twain.°

Prospero.   [*Aside*] The Duke of Milan
440   And his more braver daughter could control° thee,
If now 'twere fit to do't. At the first sight
They have changed eyes.° Delicate Ariel,
I'll set thee free for this. [*To Ferdinand*] A word,
good sir.
I fear you have done yourself some wrong.° A
word!

445 *Miranda.* Why speaks my father so ungently? This
Is the third man that e'er I saw; the first
That e'er I sighed for. Pity move my father
To be inclined my way!

Ferdinand.   O, if a virgin,
And your affection not gone forth, I'll make you
The Queen of Naples.

450 *Prospero.*   Soft, sir! One word more.
[*Aside*] They are both in either's pow'rs. But this
swift business

433 *single* (1) solitary (2) helpless   439 *son* (the only time Antonio's son is mentioned)   439 *twain* two (of these lords)   440
control refute   442 *changed eyes* i.e., fallen in love   444 *done
yourself some wrong* said what is not so

I must uneasy make, lest too light winning
Make the prize light. [*To Ferdinand*] One word
    more! I charge thee
That thou attend me. Thou dost here usurp
The name thou ow'st° not, and hast put thyself   *455*
Upon this island as a spy, to win it
From me, the lord on't.

Ferdinand.   No, as I am a man!

Miranda. There's nothing ill can dwell in such a
    temple.
If the ill spirit have so fair a house,
Good things will strive to dwell with't.

Prospero.   Follow me.   *460*
[*To Miranda*] Speak not you for him; he's a traitor.
    [*To Ferdinand*] Come!
I'll manacle thy neck and feet together;
Sea water shalt thou drink; thy food shall be
The fresh-brook mussels, withered roots, and husks
Wherein the acorn cradled. Follow!

Ferdinand.   No.   *465*
I will resist such entertainment till
Mine enemy has more pow'r.
                    He draws, and is charmed from moving.

Miranda.   O dear father,
Make not too rash a trial of him, for
He's gentle and not fearful.°

Prospero.   What, I say,
My foot my tutor?° [*To Ferdinand*] Put thy sword
    up, traitor—   *470*
Who mak'st a show but dar'st not strike, thy con-
    science
Is so possessed with guilt! Come, from thy ward!°
For I can here disarm thee with this stick°
And make thy weapon drop.

---

455 *ow'st* ownest   469 *gentle and not fearful* of noble birth and
no coward   470 *My foot my tutor* am I to be instructed by my inferior   472 *ward* fighting posture   473 *stick* i.e., his wand

Miranda.   Beseech you, father!

Prospero. Hence! Hang not on my garments.

475 *Miranda.*   Sir, have pity.
I'll be his surety.

Prospero.   Silence! One word more
Shall make me chide thee, if not hate thee. What,
An advocate for an impostor? Hush!
Thou think'st there is no more such shapes as he,
480 Having seen but him and Caliban. Foolish wench!
To th' most of men this is a Caliban,
And they to him are angels.

Miranda.   My affections
Are then most humble. I have no ambition
To see a goodlier man.

Prospero. [*To Ferdinand*] Come on, obey!
485 Thy nerves° are in their infancy again
And have no vigor in them.

Ferdinand.   So they are.
My spirits, as in a dream, are all bound up.
My father's loss, the weakness which I feel,
The wrack of all my friends, nor this man's threats
490 To whom I am subdued, are but light to me,
Might I but through my prison once a day
Behold this maid. All corners else o' th' earth
Let liberty make use of. Space enough
Have I in such a prison.

Prospero. [*Aside*] It works. [*To Ferdinand*] Come on.
[*To Ariel*] Thou hast done well, fine Ariel! [*To
495   Ferdinand*] Follow me.
[*To Ariel*] Hark what thou else shalt do me.

Miranda.   Be of comfort.
My father's of a better nature, sir,
Than he appears by speech. This is unwonted
Which now came from him.

485 *nerves* sinews

Prospero.   Thou shalt be as free
  As mountain winds; but then° exactly do   *500*
  All points of my command.

Ariel.   To th' syllable.

Prospero. [*To Ferdinand*] Come, follow. [*To Miranda*] Speak not for him.   *Exeunt.*

ACT II

Scene I. [*Another part of the island.*]

*Enter Alonso, Sebastian, Antonio, Gonzalo,
  Adrian, Francisco, and others.*

Gonzalo. Beseech you, sir, be merry. You have cause
  (So have we all) of joy; for our escape
  Is much beyond our loss. Our hint of° woe
  Is common; every day some sailor's wife,
  The master of some merchant,° and the merchant,   *5*
  Have just our theme of woe. But for the miracle,
  I mean our preservation, few in millions
  Can speak like us. Then wisely, good sir, weigh
  Our sorrow with° our comfort.

Alonso.   Prithee, peace.

Sebastian. [*Aside to Antonio*] He receives comfort   *10*
  like cold porridge.°

Antonio. [*Aside to Sebastian*] The visitor° will not
  give him o'er so.°

Sebastian. Look, he's winding up the watch of his
  wit; by and by it will strike.   *15*

500 *then* till then   II.i.3 *hint of* occasion for   5 *master of some
merchant* captain of some merchant ship   9 *with* against   10–11 *He
receives comfort like cold porridge* ("He" is Alonso; pun on
"peace," since porridge contained peas)   12 *visitor* spiritual comforter   13 *give him o'er so* release him so easily

Gonzalo. Sir—

Sebastian. [*Aside to Antonio*] One. Tell.°

Gonzalo. When every grief is entertained, that's°
offered
Comes to th' entertainer—

20   *Sebastian.* A dollar.

Gonzalo. Dolor comes to him, indeed. You have
spoken truer than you purposed.

Sebastian. You have taken it wiselier° than I meant
you should.

25   *Gonzalo.* Therefore, my lord—

Antonio. Fie, what a spendthrift is he of his tongue!

Alonso. I prithee, spare.°

Gonzalo. Well, I have done. But yet—

Sebastian. He will be talking.

30   *Antonio.* Which, of he or Adrian, for a good wager,
first° begins to crow?

Sebastian. The old cock.°

Antonio. The cock'rel.°

Sebastian. Done! The wager?

35   *Antonio.* A laughter.°

Sebastian. A match!

Adrian. Though this island seem to be desert—

Antonio. Ha, ha, ha!

Sebastian. So, you're paid.

---

17 *One. Tell* he has struck one; keep count   18 *that's* that which is
23 *wiselier* i.e., understood my pun   27 *spare* spare your words
30–31 *Which, of he or Adrian . . . first* let's wager which of the two,
Gonzalo or Adrian, will first   32 *old cock* i.e., Gonzalo   33
cock'rel young cock; i.e., Adrian   35 *laughter* the winner will have
the laugh on the loser

Adrian. Uninhabitable and almost inaccessible—   *40*

Sebastian. Yet—

Adrian. Yet—

Antonio. He could not miss't.

Adrian. It must needs be of subtle, tender, and delicate temperance.°   *45*

Antonio. Temperance was a delicate wench.

Sebastian. Ay, and a subtle, as he most learnedly delivered.

Adrian. The air breathes upon us here most sweetly.

Sebastian. As if it had lungs, and rotten ones.   *50*

Antonio. Or as 'twere perfumed by a fen.

Gonzalo. Here is everything advantageous to life.

Antonio. True; save means to live.

Sebastian. Of that there's none, or little.

Gonzalo. How lush and lusty the grass looks! How green!   *55*

Antonio. The ground indeed is tawny.

Sebastian. With an eye° of green in't.

Antonio. He misses not much.

Sebastian. No; he doth but mistake the truth totally.   *60*

Gonzalo. But the rarity of it is—which is indeed almost beyond credit—

Sebastian. As many vouched rarities are.

Gonzalo. That our garments, being, as they were, drenched in the sea, hold, notwithstanding, their   *65* freshness and glosses, being rather new-dyed than stained with salt water.

45 *temperance* climate (in the next line, a girl's name)   58 *eye* spot (also perhaps Gonzalo's eye)

Antonio. If but one of his pockets could speak, would it not say he lies?°

70 *Sebastian.* Ay, or very falsely pocket up his report.°

Gonzalo. Methinks our garments are now as fresh as when we put them on first in Afric, at the marriage of the King's fair daughter Claribel to the King of Tunis.

75 *Sebastian.* 'Twas a sweet marriage, and we prosper well in our return.

Adrian. Tunis was never graced before with such a paragon to° their queen.

Gonzalo. Not since widow Dido's time.

80 *Antonio.* Widow? A pox o' that! How came that "widow" in? Widow Dido!

Sebastian. What if he had said "widower Aeneas"° too? Good Lord, how you take it!

Adrian. "Widow Dido," said you? You make me
85 study of that. She was of Carthage, not of Tunis.

Gonzalo. This Tunis, sir, was Carthage.

Adrian. Carthage?

Gonzalo. I assure you, Carthage.

Antonio. His word is more than the miraculous
90 harp.°

Sebastian. He hath raised the wall and houses too.

Antonio. What impossible matter will he make easy next?

68–69 *If but . . . he lies* i.e., the inside of Gonzalo's pockets are stained   70 *Ay, or . . . his report* unless the pocket were, like a false knave, to receive without resentment the imputation that it is unstained   78 *to* for   81–82 *Widow Dido . . . "widower Aeneas"* (the point of the joke is that Dido was a widow, but one doesn't ordinarily think of her that way; and the same with Aeneas)   89–90 *miraculous harp* (of Amphion, which only raised the *walls* of Thebes; whereas Gonzalo has rebuilt the whole ancient city of Carthage by identifying it mistakenly with modern Tunis)

Sebastian. I think he will carry this island home in his
    pocket and give it his son for an apple.   *95*

Antonio. And, sowing the kernels of it in the sea,
    bring forth more islands.

Gonzalo. Ay!

Antonio. Why, in good time.°

Gonzalo. [*To Alonso*] Sir, we were talking that our   *100*
    garments seem now as fresh as when we were at
    Tunis at the marriage of your daughter, who is now
    Queen.

Antonio. And the rarest that e'er came there.

Sebastian. Bate,° I beseech you, widow Dido.   *105*

Antonio. O, widow Dido? Ay, widow Dido!

Gonzalo. Is not, sir, my doublet as fresh as the first
    day I wore it? I mean, in a sort.°

Antonio. That "sort" was well fished for.

Gonzalo. When I wore it at your daughter's marriage.   *110*

Alonso. You cram these words into mine ears against
    The stomach of my sense.° Would I had never
    Married my daughter there! For, coming thence,
    My son is lost; and, in my rate,° she too,
    Who is so far from Italy removed   *115*
    I ne'er again shall see her. O thou mine heir
    Of Naples and of Milan, what strange fish
    Hath made his meal on thee?

Francisco.   Sir, he may live.
    I saw him beat the surges under him
    And ride upon their backs. He trod the water,   *120*
    Whose enmity he flung aside, and breasted

99 *Why, in good time* (hearing Gonzalo reaffirm his false statement
about Tunis and Carthage, Antonio suggests that Gonzalo will indeed, at the first opportunity, carry this island home in his pocket)
105 *Bate* except   108 *in a sort* so to speak   111–12 *against/The
stomach of my sense* i.e., though my mind (or feelings) have no
appetite for them   114 *rate* opinion

The surge most swol'n that met him. His bold head
'Bove the contentious waves he kept, and oared
Himself with his good arms in lusty stroke
To th' shore, that o'er his° wave-worn basis
125   bowed,°
As stooping to relieve him. I not doubt
He came alive to land.

Alonso.   No, no, he's gone.

Sebastian. [*To Alonso*] Sir, you may thank yourself for
        this great loss,
That would not bless our Europe with your
        daughter,
130   But rather loose her to an African,
Where she, at least, is banished from your eye
Who hath cause to wet the grief on't.

Alonso.   Prithee, peace.

Sebastian. You were kneeled to and importuned
        otherwise
By all of us; and the fair soul herself
135   Weighed, between loathness and obedience, at
Which end o' th' beam should bow.° We have lost
        your son,
I fear, forever. Milan and Naples have
Moe° widows in them of this business' making
Than we bring men to comfort them.
The fault's your own.

140   *Alonso.*   So is the dear'st° o' th' loss.

Gonzalo. My Lord Sebastian,
The truth you speak doth lack some gentleness,
And time to speak it in. You rub the sore
When you should bring the plaster.

Sebastian.   Very well.

---

125 *his* its   125 *wave-worn basis bowed* (the image is of a guardian
cliff on the shore)   135–36 *Weighed, between . . . should bow*
(Claribel's unwillingness to marry was outweighed by her obedience
to her father)   138 *Moe* more   140 *dear'st* (intensifies the meaning of the noun)

Antonio. And most chirurgeonly.°   145

Gonzalo. [*To Alonso*] It is foul weather in us all, good
     sir,
  When you are cloudy.

Sebastian. [*Aside to Antonio*] Foul weather?

Antonio. [*Aside to Sebastian*]   Very foul.

Gonzalo. Had I plantation° of this isle, my lord—

Antonio. He'd sow't with nettle seed.

Sebastian.   Or docks, or mallows.

Gonzalo. And were the king on't, what would I do?   150

Sebastian. Scape being drunk for want of wine.

Gonzalo. I' th' commonwealth I would by contraries°
  Execute all things. For no kind of traffic°
  Would I admit; no name of magistrate;
  Letters° should not be known; riches, poverty,   155
  And use of service,° none; contract, succession,°
  Bourn,° bound of land, tilth,° vineyard, none;
  No use of metal, corn, or wine, or oil;
  No occupation; all men idle, all;
  And women too, but innocent and pure;
  No sovereignty.

Sebastian.   Yet he would be king on't.

Antonio. The latter end of his commonwealth forgets
  the beginning.

Gonzalo. All things in common nature should pro-
     duce
  Without sweat or endeavor. Treason, felony,   165
  Sword, pike, knife, gun, or need of any engine°
  Would I not have; but nature should bring forth,
  Of it° own kind, all foison,° all abundance,

145 *chirurgeonly* like a surgeon   148 *plantation* colonization (Antonio then puns by taking the word in its other sense)   152 *con-
traries* in contrast to the usual customs   153 *traffic* trade   155 *Letters* learning   156 *service* servants   156 *succession* inheritance
157 *Bourn* boundary   157 *tilth* agriculture   166 *engine* weapon
168 *it* its   168 *foison* abundance

To feed my innocent people.

170 *Sebastian.* No marrying 'mong his subjects?

Antonio. None, man, all idle—whores and knaves.

Gonzalo. I would with such perfection govern, sir,
    T' excel the Golden Age.

Sebastian. [*Loudly*]   Save his Majesty!

Antonio. [*Loudly*] Long live Gonzalo!

Gonzalo.   And—do you mark me, sir'

Alonso. Prithee, no more. Thou dost talk nothing to
175   me.

Gonzalo. I do well believe your Highness; and did
    it to minister occasion° to these gentlemen, who
    are of such sensible° and nimble lungs that they
    always use to laugh at nothing.

180 *Antonio.* 'Twas you we laughed at.

Gonzalo. Who in this kind of merry fooling am noth-
    ing to you; so you may continue, and laugh at
    nothing still.

Antonio. What a blow was there given!

185 *Sebastian.* And° it had not fall'n flatlong.°

Gonzalo. You are gentlemen of brave mettle; you
    would lift the moon out of her sphere if she would
    continue in it five weeks without changing.

Enter Ariel [invisible] playing solemn music.

Sebastian. We would so, and then go a-batfowling.°

190 *Antonio.* Nay, good my lord, be not angry.

177 *minister occasion* afford opportunity   178 *sensible* sensitive
185 *And* if   185 *flatlong* with the flat of the sword   189 *We would
so, and then go a-batfowling* we would use the moon for a lantern in
order to hunt birds at night by attracting them with a light and
beating them down with bats; i.e., in order to gull simpletons
like you (?)

Gonzalo. No, I warrant you; I will not adventure my
　　discretion so weakly.° Will you laugh me asleep?
　　For I am very heavy.

Antonio. Go sleep, and hear us.
　　　[*All sleep except Alonso, Sebastian, and Antonio.*]

Alonso. What, all so soon asleep? I wish mine eyes　195
　　Would, with themselves, shut up my thoughts. I
　　　find
　　They are inclined to do so.

Sebastian.　　　　　　　Please you, sir,
　　Do not omit° the heavy offer of it.
　　It seldom visits sorrow; when it doth,
　　It is a comforter.

Antonio.　　　　　　We two, my lord,　　　200
　　Will guard your person while you take your rest,
　　And watch your safety.

Alonso.　　　　　　Thank you. Wondrous heavy.
　　　[*Alonso sleeps. Exit Ariel.*]

Sebastian. What a strange drowsiness possesses them!

Antonio. It is the quality o' th' climate.

Sebastian.　　　　　　　　Why
　　Doth it not then our eyelids sink? I find not　　205
　　Myself disposed to sleep.

Antonio.　　　　　　Nor I: my spirits are nimble.
　　They fell together all, as by consent.
　　They dropped as by a thunderstroke. What might,
　　Worthy Sebastian—O, what might?—No more!
　　And yet methinks I see it in thy face,　　　210
　　What thou shouldst be. Th' occasion speaks° thee,
　　　and
　　My strong imagination sees a crown
　　Dropping upon thy head.

191–92 *adventure my discretion so weakly* risk my reputation for
good sense because of your weak wit　198 *omit* neglect　211 *speaks*
speaks to

Sebastian.   What? Art thou waking?

Antonio. Do you not hear me speak?

Sebastian.   I do; and surely
215   It is a sleepy language, and thou speak'st
      Out of thy sleep. What is it thou didst say?
      This is a strange repose, to be asleep
      With eyes wide open; standing, speaking, moving,
      And yet so fast asleep.

Antonio.   Noble Sebastian,
220   Thou let'st thy fortune sleep—die, rather; wink'st°
      Whiles thou art waking.

Sebastian.   Thou dost snore distinctly;
      There's meaning in thy snores.

Antonio. I am more serious than my custom. You
      Must be so too, if heed° me; which to do
      Trebles thee o'er.°

225 *Sebastian.*   Well, I am standing water.

Antonio. I'll teach you how to flow.

Sebastian.   Do so. To ebb
      Hereditary sloth instructs me.

Antonio.   O,
      If you but knew how you the purpose cherish
      Whiles thus you mock it; how, in stripping it,
230   You more invest it!° Ebbing men, indeed,
      Most often do so near the bottom run
      By their own fear or sloth.

Sebastian.   Prithee, say on.
      The setting of thine eye and cheek proclaim
      A matter° from thee; and a birth, indeed,
      Which throes thee much° to yield.

235 *Antonio.*   Thus, sir:

220 *wink'st* dost shut thine eyes   224 *if heed* if you heed   225
Trebles thee o'er makes thee three times what thou now art   229–
30 *in stripping . . . invest it* in stripping the purpose off you, you
clothe yourself with it all the more   234 *matter* matter of importance   235 *throes thee much* costs thee much pain

Although this lord of weak remembrance,° this
Who shall be of as little memory°
When he is earthed,° hath here almost persuaded
(For he's a spirit of persuasion, only
Professes to persuade°) the King his son's alive,   240
'Tis as impossible that he's undrowned
As he that sleeps here swims.

Sebastian.   I have no hope
That he's undrowned.

Antonio.   O, out of that no hope
What great hope have you! No hope that way is
Another way so high a hope that even   245
Ambition cannot pierce a wink beyond,
But doubt discovery there.° Will you grant with me
That Ferdinand is drowned?

Sebastian.   He's gone.

Antonio.   Then tell me,
Who's the next heir of Naples?

Sebastian.   Claribel.

Antonio. She that is Queen of Tunis; she that dwells   250
Ten leagues beyond man's life;° she that from
     Naples
Can have no note—unless the sun were post;°
The man i' th' moon's too slow—till newborn chins
Be rough and razorable;° she that from whom
We all were sea-swallowed,° though some cast°
     again,   255

236 *remembrance* memory   237 *of as little memory* as little remembered   238 *earthed* buried   239–40 *only/Professes to persuade* his
only profession is to persuade   246–47 *Ambition cannot . . . discovery there* the eye of ambition can reach no farther, but must even
doubt the reality of what it discerns thus far   251 *ten leagues beyond man's life* it would take a lifetime to get within ten leagues of
the place   252 *post* messenger   253–54 *till newborn chins/Be
rough and razorable* till babies just born be ready to shave   254–
55 *she that . . . were sea-swallowed* she who is separated from
Naples by so dangerous a sea that we were ourselves swallowed
up by it   255 *cast* cast upon the shore (with a suggestion of its
theatrical meaning that leads to the next metaphor)

And, by that destiny, to perform an act
Whereof what's past is prologue, what to come,
In yours and my discharge.

Sebastian.   What stuff is this? How say you?
'Tis true my brother's daughter's Queen of Tunis;
260 So is she heir of Naples; 'twixt which regions
There is some space.

Antonio.   A space whose ev'ry cubit
Seems to cry out "How shall that Claribel
Measure us back to Naples? Keep in Tunis,
And let Sebastian wake!" Say this were death
265   That now hath seized them, why, they were no
        worse
Than now they are. There be that can rule Naples
As well as he that sleeps; lords that can prate
As amply and unnecessarily
As this Gonzalo; I myself could make
270 A chough° of as deep chat. O, that you bore
The mind that I do! What a sleep were this
For your advancement! Do you understand me?

Sebastian. Methinks I do.

Antonio.   And how does your content
Tender° your own good fortune?

Sebastian.   I remember
You did supplant your brother Prospero.

275 *Antonio.*   True.
And look how well my garments sit upon me,
Much feater° than before. My brother's servants
Were then my fellows; now they are my men.

Sebastian. But, for your conscience—

280 *Antonio.* Ay, sir, where lies that? If 'twere a kibe,°
'Twould put me to my slipper; but I feel not
This deity in my bosom. Twenty consciences

---

270 *chough* jackdaw (a bird that can be taught to speak a few
words)   274 *Tender* regard (i.e., do you like your good fortune)
277 *feater* more becomingly   280 *kibe* chilblain on the heel

That stand 'twixt me and Milan, candied be they
And melt, ere they molest! Here lies your brother,
No better than the earth he lies upon—   285
If he were that which now he's like, that's dead°—
Whom I with this obedient steel (three inches
    of it)
Can lay to bed forever; whiles you, doing thus,
To the perpetual wink° for aye might put
This ancient morsel, this Sir Prudence, who   290
Should not upbraid our course. For all the rest,
They'll take suggestion as a cat laps milk;
They'll tell the clock° to any business that
We say befits the hour.

Sebastian.   Thy case, dear friend,
Shall be my precedent. As thou got'st Milan,   295
I'll come by Naples. Draw thy sword. One stroke
Shall free thee from the tribute which thou payest,
And I the King shall love thee.

Antonio.   Draw together;
And when I rear my hand, do you the like,
To fall it on Gonzalo.   [*They draw.*]

Sebastian.   O, but one word!   300

Enter Ariel [*invisible*] *with music and song.*

Ariel. My master through his art foresees the danger
That you, his friend, are in, and sends me forth
(For else his project dies) to keep them living.
                        Sings in Gonzalo's ear.

            While you here do snoring lie,
            Open-eyed conspiracy   305
                His time doth take.
            If of life you keep a care,
            Shake off slumber and beware.
                Awake, awake!

286 *that's dead* that is, if he were dead   289 *wink* eye-shut   293
tell the clock say yes

Antonio. Then let us both be sudden.

310 *Gonzalo.* [*Wakes*]   Now good angels
    Preserve the King!   [*The others wake.*]

Alonso. Why, how now? Ho, awake! Why are you
    drawn?
    Wherefore this ghastly looking?

Gonzalo.   What's the matter?

Sebastian. Whiles we stood here securing your repose,
315 Even now, we heard a hollow burst of bellowing
    Like bulls, or rather lions. Did't not wake you?
    It struck mine ear most terribly.

Alonso.   I heard nothing.

Antonio. O, 'twas a din to fright a monster's ear,
    To make an earthquake! Sure it was the roar
    Of a whole herd of lions.

320 *Alonso.*   Heard you this, Gonzalo?

Gonzalo. Upon mine honor, sir, I heard a humming,
    And that a strange one too, which did awake me.
    I shaked you, sir, and cried. As mine eyes opened,
    I saw their weapons drawn. There was a noise,
325 That's verily.° 'Tis best we stand upon our guard,
    Or that we quit this place. Let's draw our weapons.

Alonso. Lead off this ground, and let's make further
    search
    For my poor son.

Gonzalo.   Heavens keep him from these beasts!
    For he is, sure, i' th' island.

Alonso.   Lead away.

330 *Ariel.* Prospero my lord shall know what I have done.
    So, King, go safely on to seek thy son.   *Exeunt.*

325 *verily* the truth

Scene II. [*Another part of the island.*]

Enter Caliban with a burden of wood. A noise of
   thunder heard.

Caliban. All the infections that the sun sucks up
   From bogs, fens, flats, on Prosper fall, and make
      him
   By inchmeal° a disease! His spirits hear me,
   And yet I needs must curse. But they'll nor pinch,
   Fright me with urchin shows,° pitch me i' th' mire,   *5*
   Nor lead me, like a firebrand,° in the dark
   Out of my way, unless he bid 'em. But
   For every trifle are they set upon me;
   Sometime like apes that mow° and chatter at me,
   And after bite me; then like hedgehogs which   *10*
   Lie tumbling in my barefoot way and mount
   Their pricks at my footfall; sometime am I
   All wound with adders, who with cloven tongues
   Do hiss me into madness.

Enter Trinculo.

                  Lo, now, lo!
   Here comes a spirit of his, and to torment me   *15*
   For bringing wood in slowly. I'll fall flat.
   Perchance he will not mind me.   [*Lies down.*]

Trinculo. Here's neither bush nor shrub to bear off°
   any weather at all, and another storm brewing; I
   hear it sing i' th' wind. Yond same black cloud,   *20*
   yond huge one, looks like a foul bombard° that
   would shed his liquor. If it should thunder as it

II.ii.3 *By inchmeal* inch by inch   5 *urchin shows* impish apparitions
6 *like a firebrand* in the form of a will-o'-the-wisp   9 *mow* make
faces   18 *bear off* ward off   21 *bombard* large leather jug

did before, I know not where to hide my head.
Yond same cloud cannot choose but fall by pail-
25 fuls. What have we here? A man or a fish? Dead
or alive? A fish! He smells like a fish; a very ancient and fishlike smell; a kind of not of the new-
est Poor John.° A strange fish! Were I in England
now, as once I was, and had but this fish painted,°
30 not a holiday fool there but would give a piece of
silver. There would this monster make a man;° any
strange beast there makes a man. When they will
not give a doit° to relieve a lame beggar, they will
lay out ten to see a dead Indian. Legged like a man!
35 And his fins like arms! Warm, o' my troth! I do
now let loose my opinion, hold it no longer. This
is no fish, but an islander, that hath lately suffered
by a thunderbolt. [*Thunder.*] Alas, the storm is
come again! My best way is to creep under his
40 gaberdine; there is no other shelter hereabout. Misery acquaints a man with strange bedfellows. I will
here shroud till the dregs of the storm be past.

[*Creeps under Caliban's garment.*]

Enter Stephano, singing, [a bottle in his hand.]

Stephano.   I shall no more to sea, to sea;
                  Here shall I die ashore.

45 This is a very scurvy tune to sing at a man's fu-
neral. Well, here's my comfort.   *Drinks.*

           The master, the swabber, the boatswain, and I,
                  The gunner, and his mate,
           Loved Mall, Meg, and Marian, and Margery,
50   But none of us cared for Kate.
                  For she had a tongue with a tang,
                  Would cry to a sailor "Go hang!"
           She loved not the savor of tar nor of pitch;

28 *Poor John* dried hake   29 *painted* i.e., as a sign hung outside
a booth at a fair   31 *make a man* (pun: make a man's fortune)
33 *doit* smallest coin

Yet a tailor might scratch her where'er she did itch.
Then to sea, boys, and let her go hang!   *55*

This is a scurvy tune too; but here's my comfort.
                                        Drinks.

Caliban. Do not torment me! O!

Stephano. What's the matter? Have we devils here?
Do you put tricks upon 's with savages and men
of Inde, ha? I have not scaped drowning to be   *60*
afeard now of your four legs. For it hath been
said, "As proper a man as ever went on four legs
cannot make him give ground"; and it shall be said
so again, while Stephano breathes at' nostrils.°

Caliban. The spirit torments me. O!   *65*

Stephano. This is some monster of the isle, with four
legs, who hath got, as I take it, an ague. Where the
devil should he learn our language? I will give him
some relief, if it be but for that. If I can recover°
him, and keep him tame, and get to Naples with   *70*
him, he's a present for any emperor that ever trod
on neat's leather.°

Caliban. Do not torment me, prithee; I'll bring my
wood home faster.

Stephano. He's in his fit now and does not talk after   *75*
the wisest. He shall taste of my bottle; if he have
never drunk wine afore, it will go near to remove
his fit. If I can recover him and keep him tame, I
will not take too much° for him. He shall pay for
him that hath him, and that soundly.   *80*

Caliban. Thou dost me yet but little hurt. Thou wilt
anon;° I know it by thy trembling.° Now Prosper
works upon thee.

Stephano. Come on your ways, open your mouth;

64 *at' nostrils* at the nostrils   69 *recover* cure   72 *neat's leather*
cowhide   79 *not take too much* too much will not be enough
82 *anon* soon   82 *trembling* (Trinculo is shaking with fear)

85   here is that which will give language to you, cat.°
    Open your mouth. This will shake your shaking, I
    can tell you, and that soundly. [*Gives Caliban
    drink.*] You cannot tell who's your friend. Open
    your chaps° again.

90 *Trinculo.* I should know that voice. It should be—
    but he is drowned; and these are devils. O, defend
    me!

   Stephano. Four legs and two voices—a most delicate
    monster! His forward voice now is to speak well
95   of his friend; his backward voice is to utter foul
    speeches and to detract. If all the wine in my bottle
    will recover him, I will help his ague. Come! [*Gives
    drink.*] Amen! I will pour some in thy other
    mouth.

100 *Trinculo.* Stephano!

   Stephano. Doth thy other mouth call me? Mercy,
    mercy! This is a devil, and no monster. I will leave
    him; I have no long spoon.°

   Trinculo. Stephano! If thou beest Stephano, touch me
105   and speak to me; for I am Trinculo—be not afeard
    —thy good friend Trinculo.

   Stephano. If thou beest Trinculo, come forth. I'll pull
    thee by the lesser legs. If any be Trinculo's legs,
    these are they. [*Draws him out from under Cali-*
110   *ban's garment.*] Thou art very Trinculo indeed!
    How cam'st thou to be the siege° of this moon-
    calf?° Can he vent Trinculos?

   Trinculo. I took him to be killed with a thunder-
    stroke. But art thou not drowned, Stephano? I
115   hope now thou art not drowned. Is the storm over-
    blown? I hid me under the dead mooncalf's gaber-
    dine for fear of the storm. And art thou living,

85 *cat* (alluding to the proverb "Liquor will make a cat talk")
89 *chaps* jaws   103 *long spoon* (alluding to the proverb "He who
sups with [i.e., from the same dish as] the devil must have a long
spoon")   111 *siege* excrement   111-12 *mooncalf* monstrosity

Stephano? O Stephano, two Neapolitans scaped!

Stephano. Prithee do not turn me about; my stomach
   is not constant.   120

Caliban. [*Aside*] These be fine things, and if° they be
    not sprites.
   That's a brave god and bears celestial liquor.
   I will kneel to him.

Stephano. How didst thou scape? How cam'st thou
   hither? Swear by this bottle how thou cam'st   125
   hither. I escaped upon a butt of sack which the
   sailors heaved o'erboard—by this bottle which I
   made of the bark of a tree with mine own hands
   since I was cast ashore.

Caliban. I'll swear upon that bottle to be thy true   130
   subject, for the liquor is not earthly.

Stephano. Here! Swear then how thou escap'dst.

Trinculo. Swum ashore, man, like a duck. I can swim
   like a duck, I'll be sworn.

Stephano. Here, kiss the book. [*Gives him drink.*]   135
   Though thou canst swim like a duck, thou art made
   like a goose.

Trinculo. O Stephano, hast any more of this?

Stephano. The whole butt, man. My cellar is in a
   rock by th' seaside, where my wine is hid. How   140
   now, mooncalf? How does thine ague?

Caliban. Hast thou not dropped from heaven?

Stephano. Out o' th' moon, I do assure thee. I was the
   Man i' th' Moon when time was.°

Caliban. I have seen thee in her, and I do adore thee.   145
   My mistress showed me thee, and thy dog, and
   thy bush.°

121 *and if* if   144 *when time was* once upon a time   146–47 *thee,
and thy dog, and thy bush* (the Man in the Moon was banished
there, according to legend, for gathering brushwood with his dog
on Sunday)

Stephano. Come, swear to that; kiss the book. [*Gives him drink.*] I will furnish it anon with new con-
150   tents. Swear. [*Caliban drinks.*]

Trinculo. By this good light, this is a very shallow monster! I afeard of him? A very weak monster! The Man i' th' Moon? A most poor credulous monster! Well drawn,° monster, in good sooth!

155 *Caliban.* I'll show thee every fertile inch o' th' island; and I will kiss thy foot. I prithee, be my god.

Trinculo. By this light, a most perfidious and drunken monster! When's god's asleep, he'll rob his bottle.

Caliban. I'll kiss thy foot. I'll swear myself thy sub-
160   ject.

Stephano. Come on then. Down, and swear!

Trinculo. I shall laugh myself to death at this puppy-headed monster. A most scurvy monster! I could find in my heart to beat him—

165 *Stephano.* Come, kiss.

Trinculo. But that the poor monster's in drink. An abominable monster!

Caliban. I'll show thee the best springs; I'll pluck thee berries;
  I'll fish for thee, and get thee wood enough.
170 A plague upon the tyrant that I serve!
  I'll bear him no more sticks, but follow thee,
  Thou wondrous man.

Trinculo. A most ridiculous monster, to make a wonder of a poor drunkard!

Caliban. I prithee let me bring thee where crabs°
175   grow;
  And I with my long nails will dig thee pignuts,°
  Show thee a jay's nest, and instruct thee how

154 *Well drawn* a good pull at the bottle   175 *crabs* crab apples
176 *pignuts* earthnuts

To snare the nimble marmoset. I'll bring thee
To clust'ring filberts, and sometimes I'll get thee
Young scamels° from the rock. Wilt thou go with
   me?   *180*

Stephano. I prithee now, lead the way without any
   more talking. Trinculo, the King and all our company else being drowned, we will inherit here.
   Here, bear my bottle. Fellow Trinculo, we'll fill
   him by and by again.   *185*
                         Caliban sings drunkenly.

Caliban. Farewell, master; farewell, farewell!

Trinculo. A howling monster! A drunken monster!

Caliban.
        No more dams° I'll make for fish,
           Nor fetch in firing
           At requiring,   *190*
        Nor scrape trenchering,° nor wash dish.
           'Ban, 'Ban, Ca—Caliban
        Has a new master. Get a new man!

   Freedom, high day! High day, freedom! Freedom,
   high day, freedom!   *195*

Stephano. O brave monster! Lead the way.   *Exeunt.*

ACT III

Scene I. [*In front of Prospero's cell.*]

Enter Ferdinand, bearing a log.

Ferdinand. There be some sports are painful, and
   their labor
Delight in them sets off;° some kinds of baseness

---

180 *scamels* (perhaps a misprint for "seamels" or "seamews," a
kind of sea bird)   188 *dams* (to catch fish and keep them)   191
trenchering trenchers, wooden plates   III.i.2 *sets off* cancels

Are nobly undergone, and most poor matters
Point to rich ends. This my mean task
5 Would be as heavy to me as odious, but
The mistress which I serve quickens° what's dead
And makes my labors pleasures. O, she is
Ten times more gentle than her father's crabbed;
And he's composed of harshness. I must remove
10 Some thousands of these logs and pile them up,
Upon a sore injunction.° My sweet mistress
Weeps when she sees me work, and says such
  baseness
Had never like executor. I forget;°
But these sweet thoughts do even refresh my
  labors,
Most busiest when I do it.°

Enter Miranda; and Prospero [behind, unseen].

15 *Miranda.*   Alas, now pray you,
Work not so hard! I would the lightning had
Burnt up those logs that you are enjoined to pile!
Pray set it down and rest you. When this burns,
'Twill weep° for having wearied you. My father
20 Is hard at study; pray now rest yourself;
He's safe for these three hours.

Ferdinand.   O most dear mistress,
The sun will set before I shall discharge
What I must strive to do.

Miranda.   If you'll sit down,
I'll bear your logs the while. Pray give me that;
I'll carry it to the pile.

25 *Ferdinand.*   No, precious creature,
I had rather crack my sinews, break my back,
Than you should such dishonor undergo
While I sit lazy by.

6 *quickens* brings to life 11 *sore injunction* severe command
13 *forget* i.e., my task 15 *Most busiest when I do it* i.e., my
thoughts are busiest when I am (the Folio's *busie lest* has been
variously emended; *it* may refer to "task," line 4, the understood
object in line 13) 19 *weep* i.e., exude resin

Miranda.   It would become me
  As well as it does you; and I should do it
  With much more ease; for my good will is to it,   30
  And yours it is against.

Prospero. [*Aside*]   Poor worm, thou art infected!
  This visitation° shows it.

Miranda.   You look wearily.

Ferdinand. No, noble mistress, 'tis fresh morning with
    me
  When you are by at night.° I do beseech you,
  Chiefly that I might set it in my prayers,   35
  What is your name?

Miranda.   Miranda. O my father,
  I have broke your hest° to say so!

Ferdinand.   Admired Miranda!°
  Indeed the top of admiration, worth
  What's dearest to the world! Full many a lady
  I have eyed with best regard, and many a time   40
  Th' harmony of their tongues hath into bondage
  Brought my too diligent ear. For several virtues
  Have I liked several women; never any
  With so full soul but some defect in her
  Did quarrel with the noblest grace she owed,°   45
  And put it to the foil.° But you, O you,
  So perfect and so peerless, are created
  Of every creature's best.

Miranda.   I do not know
  One of my sex; no woman's face remember,
  Save, from my glass, mine own. Nor have I seen   50
  More that I may call men than you, good friend,
  And my dear father. How features are abroad
  I am skilless° of; but, by my modesty

32 *visitation* (1) visit (2) attack of plague (referring to metaphor
of "infected")   34 *at night* i.e., even at night when I am very
tired   37 *hest* command   37 *Admired Miranda* ("admired" means
"to be wondered at"; the Latin "Miranda" means "wonderful")
45 *owed* owned   46 *put it to the foil* defeated it   53 *skilless*
ignorant

(The jewel in my dower), I would not wish
55 Any companion in the world but you;
Nor can imagination form a shape,
Besides yourself, to like of.° But I prattle
Something too wildly, and my father's precepts
I therein do forget.

Ferdinand.   I am, in my condition,
60 A prince, Miranda; I do think, a king
(I would not so), and would no more endure
This wooden slavery than to suffer
The fleshfly blow my mouth. Hear my soul speak!
The very instant that I saw you, did
65 My heart fly to your service; there resides,
To make me slave to it; and for your sake
Am I this patient log-man.

Miranda.   Do you love me?

Ferdinand. O heaven, O earth, bear witness to this
        sound,
And crown what I profess with kind event°
70 If I speak true! If hollowly, invert
What best is boded me° to mischief! I,
Beyond all limit of what else i' th' world,
Do love, prize, honor you.

Miranda.   I am a fool
To weep at what I am glad of.

Prospero.   [*Aside*] Fair encounter
75 Of two most rare affections! Heavens rain grace
On that which breeds between 'em!

Ferdinand.   Wherefore weep you?

Miranda. At mine unworthiness, that dare not offer
What I desire to give, and much less take
What I shall die to want.° But this is trifling;°
80 And all the more it seeks to hide itself,

57 *like of* like   69 *event* outcome   71 *What best is boded me* whatever good fortune fate has in store for me   79 *to want* if I lack
79 *trifling* i.e., to speak in riddles like this

The bigger bulk it shows. Hence, bashful cunning,
And prompt me, plain and holy innocence!
I am your wife, if you will marry me;
If not, I'll die your maid. To be your fellow°
You may deny me; but I'll be your servant,   85
Whether you will or no.

Ferdinand.   My mistress, dearest,
And I thus humble ever.

Miranda.   My husband then?

Ferdinand. Ay, with a heart as willing
As bondage e'er of freedom.° Here's my hand.

Miranda. And mine, with my heart in't; and now
      farewell   90
Till half an hour hence.

Ferdinand.   A thousand thousand!
                    *Exeunt [Ferdinand and Miranda
                          in different directions].*

Prospero. So glad of this as they I cannot be,
Who are surprised withal;° but my rejoicing
At nothing can be more. I'll to my book;
For yet ere suppertime must I perform   95
Much business appertaining.°   *Exit.*

Scene II. [*Another part of the island.*]

Enter Caliban, Stephano, and Trinculo.

Stephano. Tell not me! When the butt is out, we will
      drink water; not a drop before. Therefore bear up
      and board 'em!° Servant monster, drink to me.

Trinculo. Servant monster? The folly of this island!

84 *fellow* equal 89 *of freedom* i.e., to win freedom 93 *withal* by
it 96 *appertaining* i.e., to my plan III.ii.2–3 *bear up and board
'em* i.e., drink up

5   They say there's but five upon this isle; we are three
of them. If th' other two be brained like us, the
state totters.

Stephano. Drink, servant monster, when I bid thee;
thy eyes are almost set in thy head.

10 *Trinculo.* Where should they be set else? He were a
brave monster indeed if they were set in his tail.

Stephano. My man-monster hath drowned his tongue
in sack. For my part, the sea cannot drown me. I
swam, ere I could recover the shore, five-and-thirty
15   leagues off and on, by this light. Thou shalt be my
lieutenant, monster, or my standard.°

Trinculo. Your lieutenant, if you list;° he's no standard.

Stephano. We'll not run,° Monsieur Monster.

20 *Trinculo.* Nor go° neither; but you'll lie° like dogs,
and yet say nothing neither.

Stephano. Mooncalf, speak once in thy life, if thou
beest a good mooncalf.

Caliban. How does thy honor? Let me lick thy shoe.
25   I'll not serve him; he is not valiant.

Trinculo. Thou liest, most ignorant monster; I am in
case° to justle° a constable. Why, thou deboshed°
fish thou, was there ever man a coward that hath
drunk so much sack as I today? Wilt thou tell a
30   monstrous lie, being but half a fish and half a
monster?

Caliban. Lo, how he mocks me! Wilt thou let him,
my lord?

---

16 *standard* standard-bearer, ensign (pun since Caliban is so drunk
he cannot stand)   17 *if you list* if it please you (with pun on
"list" as pertaining to a ship that leans over to one side)   19–20
run, lie (with puns on secondary meanings: "make water," "ex-
crete")   20 *go* walk   27 *case* fit condition   27 *justle* jostle   27 *de-
boshed* debauched

Trinculo. "Lord" quoth he? That a monster should
  be such a natural!°   35

Caliban. Lo, lo, again! Bite him to death, I prithee.

Stephano. Trinculo, keep a good tongue in your head.
  If you prove a mutineer—the next tree!° The poor
  monster's my subject, and he shall not suffer in-
  dignity.   40

Caliban. I thank my noble lord. Wilt thou be pleased
  to hearken once again to the suit I made to thee?

Stephano. Marry,° will I. Kneel and repeat it; I will
  stand, and so shall Trinculo.

Enter Ariel, invisible.

Caliban. As I told thee before, I am subject to a
  tyrant,   45
  A sorcerer, that by his cunning hath
  Cheated me of the island.

Ariel. Thou liest.

Caliban.   Thou liest, thou jesting monkey
  thou!
  I would my valiant master would destroy thee.
  I do not lie.   50

Stephano. Trinculo, if you trouble him any more in's
  tale, by this hand, I will supplant some of your
  teeth.

Trinculo. Why, I said nothing.

Stephano. Mum then, and no more. Proceed.   55

Caliban. I say by sorcery he got this isle;
  From me he got it. If thy greatness will
  Revenge it on him—for I know thou dar'st,
  But this thing° dare not—

35 *natural* idiot 38 *the next tree* i.e., you will be hanged 43
Marry (an expletive, from "By the Virgin Mary") 59 *this thing*
i.e., Trinculo

60 *Stephano.* That's most certain.

Caliban. Thou shalt be lord of it, and I'll serve thee.

Stephano. How now shall this be compassed?
Canst thou bring me to the party?

Caliban. Yea, yea, my lord! I'll yield him thee asleep,
65 Where thou mayst knock a nail into his head.

Ariel. Thou liest; thou canst not.

Caliban. What a pied° ninny's this! Thou scurvy
patch!°
I do beseech thy greatness, give him blows
And take his bottle from him. When that's gone,
He shall drink naught but brine, for I'll not show
70 him
Where the quick freshes° are.

Stephano. Trinculo, run into no further danger! Interrupt the monster one word further and, by this
hand, I'll turn my mercy out o' doors and make a
75 stockfish° of thee.

Trinculo. Why, what did I? I did nothing. I'll go farther off.

Stephano. Didst thou not say he lied?

Ariel. Thou liest.

80 *Stephano.* Do I so? Take thou that! [*Strikes Trinculo.*] As you like this, give me the lie another time.

Trinculo. I did not give the lie. Out o' your wits, and
hearing too? A pox o' your bottle! This can sack
and drinking do. A murrain° on your monster, and
85 the devil take your fingers!

Caliban. Ha, ha, ha!

Stephano. Now forward with your tale. [*To Trinculo*]
Prithee, stand further off.

---

67 *pied* (referring to Trinculo's parti-colored jester's costume)
67 *patch* clown 71 *quick freshes* living springs of fresh water
75 *stockfish* dried cod, softened by beating 84 *murrain* plague
(that infects cattle)

Caliban. Beat him enough. After a little time
   I'll beat him too.

Stephano.   Stand farther. Come, proceed.   *90*

Caliban. Why, as I told thee, 'tis a custom with him
   I' th' afternoon to sleep. There thou mayst brain
    him,
   Having first seized his books, or with a log
   Batter his skull, or paunch° him with a stake,
   Or cut his wezand° with thy knife. Remember   *95*
   First to possess his books; for without them
   He's but a sot,° as I am, nor hath not
   One spirit to command. They all do hate him
   As rootedly as I. Burn but his books.
   He has brave utensils° (for so he calls them)   *100*
   Which, when he has a house, he'll deck withal.
   And that most deeply to consider is
   The beauty of his daughter. He himself
   Calls her a nonpareil. I never saw a woman
   But only Sycorax my dam and she;   *105*
   But she as far surpasseth Sycorax
   As great'st does least.

Stephano.   Is it so brave a lass?

Caliban. Ay, lord. She will become thy bed, I
   warrant,
   And bring thee forth brave brood.

Stephano. Monster, I will kill this man. His daughter   *110*
   and I will be King and Queen—save our Graces!—
   and Trinculo and thyself shall be viceroys. Dost
   thou like the plot, Trinculo?

Trinculo. Excellent.

Stephano. Give me thy hand. I am sorry I beat thee;   *115*
   but while thou liv'st, keep a good tongue in thy
   head.

94 *paunch* stab in the belly 95 *wezand* windpipe 97 *sot* fool
100 *brave utensils* fine furnishings (pronounced "útensils")

Caliban. Within this half hour will he be asleep.
    Wilt thou destroy him then?

Stephano.   Ay, on mine honor.

120 *Ariel.* This will I tell my master.

Caliban. Thou mak'st me merry; I am full of pleasure.
    Let us be jocund. Will you troll the catch°
    You taught me but whilere?°

Stephano. At thy request, monster, I will do reason,
125   any reason.° Come on, Trinculo, let us sing. *Sings.*

              Flout 'em and scout° 'em
              And scout 'em and flout 'em!
              Thought is free.

Caliban. That's not the tune.
        Ariel plays the tune on a tabor° and pipe.

130 *Stephano.* What is this same?

Trinculo. This is the tune of our catch, played by the
    picture of Nobody.°

Stephano. If thou beest a man, show thyself in thy
    likeness. If thou beest a devil, take't as thou list.

135 *Trinculo.* O, forgive me my sins!

Stephano. He that dies pays all debts. I defy thee.
    Mercy upon us!

Caliban. Art thou afeard?

Stephano. No, monster, not I.

140 *Caliban.* Be not afeard; the isle is full of noises,
    Sounds and sweet airs that give delight and hurt
    not.

---

122 *troll the catch* sing the round   123 *but whilere* just now
124–25 *reason, any reason* i.e., anything within reason   126 *scout*
jeer at   129 s.d. *tabor* small drum worn at the side   132 *Nobody*
(alluding to the picture of No-body—a man all head, legs, and arms,
but without trunk—on the title page of the anonymous comedy
No-body and Some-body)

Sometimes a thousand twangling instruments
Will hum about mine ears; and sometime voices
That, if I then had waked after long sleep,
Will make me sleep again; and then, in dreaming,   145
The clouds methought would open and show riches
Ready to drop upon me, that, when I waked,
I cried to dream again.

Stephano. This will prove a brave kingdom to me,
where I shall have my music for nothing.   150

Caliban. When Prospero is destroyed.

Stephano. That shall be by and by; I remember the
story.

Trinculo. The sound is going away; let's follow it, and
after do our work.   155

Stephano. Lead, monster; we'll follow. I would I
could see this taborer; he lays it on.

Trinculo. [*To Caliban*] Wilt come?° I'll follow Stephano.   *Exeunt.*

Scene III. [*Another part of the island.*]

*Enter Alonso, Sebastian, Antonio, Gonzalo,
Adrian, Francisco, etc.*

Gonzalo. By'r Lakin,° I can go no further, sir;
My old bones aches. Here's a maze trod indeed
Through forthrights and meanders.° By your
     patience,
I needs must rest me.

Alonso.   Old lord, I cannot blame thee,
Who am myself attached° with weariness   5

158 *Wilt come* (Caliban lingers because the other two are being
distracted from his purpose by the music) III.iii.1 *By'r Lakin*
by our Lady 3 *forthrights and meanders* straight and winding paths
5 *attached* seized

To th' dulling of my spirits. Sit down and rest.
Even here I will put off my hope, and keep it
No longer for my flatterer. He is drowned
Whom thus we stray to find; and the sea mocks
10   Our frustrate search on land. Well, let him go.

Antonio. [*Aside to Sebastian*] I am right glad that
        he's so out of hope.
Do not for one repulse forgo the purpose
That you resolved t' effect.

Sebastian. [*Aside to Antonio*] The next advantage
Will we take throughly.°

Antonio. [*Aside to Sebastian*] Let it be tonight;
15   For, now they are oppressed with travel, they
Will not nor cannot use such vigilance
As when they are fresh.

Sebastian. [*Aside to Antonio*] I say tonight. No more.

*Solemn and strange music; and Prosper on the top°
(invisible). Enter several strange Shapes, bringing
in a banquet; and dance about it with gentle ac-
tions of salutations; and, inviting the King etc. to
eat, they depart.*

Alonso. What harmony is this? My good friends,
        hark!

Gonzalo. Marvelous sweet music!

Alonso. Give us kind keepers,° heavens! What were
20   these?

Sebastian. A living drollery.° Now I will believe
That there are unicorns; that in Arabia

14 *throughly* thoroughly   17 s.d. *the top* upper stage (or perhaps a
playing area above it)   20 *kind keepers* guardian angels   21 *drollery* puppet show

There is one tree, the phoenix' throne; one phoenix
At this hour reigning there.

Antonio.   I'll believe both;
And what does else want credit,° come to me,   25
And I'll be sworn 'tis true. Travelers ne'er did lie,
Though fools at home condemn 'em.

Gonzalo.   If in Naples
I should report this now, would they believe me
If I should say I saw such islanders?
(For certes these are people of the island)   30
Who, though they are of monstrous shape, yet note,
Their manners are more gentle, kind, than of
Our human generation you shall find
Many—nay, almost any.

   Prospero.   [*Aside*] Honest lord,
Thou hast said well; for some of you there present   35
Are worse than devils.

Alonso.   I cannot too much muse°
Such shapes, such gesture, and such sound, ex-
   pressing
(Although they want the use of tongue) a kind
   Of excellent dumb discourse.

   Prospero.   [*Aside*] Praise in departing.°

Francisco. They vanished strangely.

Sebastian.   No matter, since   40
They have left their viands behind; for we have
   stomachs.
Will't please you taste of what is here?

Alonso.   Not I.

Gonzalo. Faith, sir, you need not fear. When we were
   boys,
Who would believe that there were mountaineers

25 *credit* believing   36 *muse* wonder at   39 *Praise in departing*
save your praise for the end

Dewlapped° like bulls, whose throats had hanging
at 'em
45   Wallets of flesh? Or that there were such men
Whose heads stood in their breasts? Which now
we find
Each putter-out of five for one° will bring us
Good warrant of.

Alonso.   I will stand to, and feed;
50   Although my last, no matter, since I feel
The best is past. Brother, my lord the Duke,
Stand to, and do as we.

*Thunder and lightning. Enter Ariel, like a harpy;
claps his wings upon the table; and with a
quaint device° the banquet vanishes.*

Ariel. You are three men of sin, whom destiny—
That hath to instrument° this lower world
55   And what is in't—the never-surfeited sea
Hath caused to belch up you and on this island,
Where man doth not inhabit, you 'mongst men
Being most unfit to live. I have made you mad;
And even with suchlike valor° men hang and
drown
Their proper selves.

[*Alonso, Sebastian, etc. draw their swords.*]
60   You fools! I and my fellows
Are ministers of Fate. The elements,
Of whom your swords are tempered,° may as well
Wound the loud winds, or with bemocked-at stabs
Kill the still-closing° waters, as diminish
One dowle° that's in my plume.° My fellow min-
65   isters

45 *Dewlapped* with skin hanging from the neck (like mountaineers
with goiter)   48 *putter-out of five for one* traveler who insures
himself by depositing a sum of money to be repaid fivefold if he
returns safely (i.e., any ordinary traveler will confirm nowadays
those reports we used to think fanciful)   52 s.d. *quaint device*
ingenious device (of stage mechanism)   54 *to instrument* as its instrument   59 *suchlike valor* i.e., the courage that comes of madness
62 *tempered* composed   64 *still-closing* ever closing again (as
soon as wounded)   65 *dowle* bit of down   65 *plume* plumage

Are like invulnerable. If you could hurt,°
Your swords are now too massy° for your strengths
And will not be uplifted. But remember
(For that's my business to you) that you three
From Milan did supplant good Prospero;   70
Exposed unto the sea, which hath requit it,°
Him and his innocent child; for which foul deed
The pow'rs, delaying, not forgetting, have
Incensed the seas and shores, yea, all the creatures,
Against your peace. Thee of thy son, Alonso,   75
They have bereft; and do pronounce by me
Ling'ring perdition (worse than any death
Can be at once) shall step by step attend
You and your ways; whose wraths to guard you
    from,
Which here, in this most desolate isle, else falls   80
Upon your heads, is nothing but heart's sorrow°
And a clear life ensuing.

*He vanishes in thunder; then, to soft music, enter
the Shapes again, and dance with mocks and
mows,° and carrying out the table.*

Prospero. Bravely the figure of this harpy hast thou
Performed, my Ariel; a grace it had, devouring.°
Of my instruction hast thou nothing bated°   85
In what thou hadst to say. So, with good life°
And observation strange,° my meaner ministers°
Their several kinds have done.° My high charms
    work,
And these, mine enemies, are all knit up
In their distractions. They now are in my pow'r;   90
And in these fits I leave them, while I visit

66 *If you could hurt* even if you could hurt us   67 *massy* heavy
71 *requit it* avenged that crime   81 *nothing but heart's sorrow* only
repentance (will protect you from the wrath of these powers)
82 s.d. *mocks and mows* mocking gestures and grimaces   84 *devouring* i.e., in making the banquet disappear   85 *bated* omitted   86
good life good lifelike acting   87 *observation strange* remarkable
attention to my wishes   87 *meaner ministers* i.e., inferior to Ariel
88 *Their several kinds have done* have acted the parts their natures
suited them for

Young Ferdinand, whom they suppose is drowne
And his and mine loved darling.   [Exit above

Gonzalo. I' th' name of something holy, sir, wh
     stand you
In this strange stare?

95 Alonso.   O, it is monstrous, monstrou
Methought the billows spoke and told me of it;
The winds did sing it to me; and the thunder,
That deep and dreadful organ pipe, pronounced
The name of Prosper; it did bass my trespass.°
100 Therefore my son i' th' ooze is bedded; and
I'll seek him deeper than e'er plummet sounded
And with him there lie mudded.   Exi

Sebastian.   But one fiend at a time
I'll fight their legions o'er!°

Antonio.   I'll be thy second.
                    Exeunt [Sebastian and Antonio]

Gonzalo. All three of them are desperate; their grea
     guilt,
105 Like poison given to work a great time after,
Now 'gins to bite the spirits. I do beseech you,
That are of suppler joints, follow them swiftly
And hinder them from what this ecstasy°
May now provoke them to.

Adrian.   Follow, I pray you.
                    Exeunt omnes

---

99 bass my trespass i.e., made me understand my trespass by turning it into music for which the thunder provided the bass par
103 o'er one after another to the last   108 ecstasy madness

ACT IV

Scene I. [*In front of Prospero's cell.*]

Enter Prospero, Ferdinand, and Miranda.

Prospero. If I have too austerely punished you,
  Your compensation makes amends; for I
  Have given you here a third of mine own life,
  Or that for which I live; who once again
  I tender to thy hand. All thy vexations   *5*
  Were but my trials of thy love, and thou
  Hast strangely° stood the test. Here, afore heaven,
  I ratify this my rich gift. O Ferdinand,
  Do not smile at me that I boast her off,°
  For thou shalt find she will outstrip all praise   *10*
  And make it halt° behind her.

Ferdinand.   I do believe it
  Against an oracle.°

Prospero. Then, as my gift, and thine own acquisition
  Worthily purchased, take my daughter. But
  If thou dost break her virgin-knot before   *15*
  All sanctimonious° ceremonies may
  With full and holy rite be minist'red,

IV.i.7 *strangely* wonderfully **9** *boast her off* (includes perhaps idea
of showing her off) **11** *halt* limp **12** *Against an oracle* though an
oracle should declare otherwise **16** *sanctimonious* holy

No sweet aspersion° shall the heavens let fall
To make this contract grow;° but barren hate,
20 Sour-eyed disdain, and discord shall bestrew
The union of your bed with weeds so loathly
That you shall hate it both. Therefore take heed,
As Hymen's lamps shall light you.°

Ferdinand.   As I hope
For quiet days, fair issue, and long life,
25 With such love as 'tis now, the murkiest den,
The most opportune° place, the strong'st sug-
      gestion
Our worser genius can,° shall never melt
Mine honor into lust, to take away
The edge° of that day's celebration
When I shall think or Phoebus' steeds are foun-
30 dered°
Or Night kept chained below.°

Prospero.   Fairly spoke.
Sit then and talk with her; she is thine own.
What, Ariel!° My industrious servant, Ariel!

Enter Ariel.

Ariel. What would my potent master? Here I am.

Prospero. Thou and thy meaner fellows your last
35 service
Did worthily perform; and I must use you
In such another trick. Go bring the rabble,°
O'er whom I give thee pow'r, here to this place.
Incite them to quick motion; for I must

18 *aspersion* blessing (like rain on crops)   19 *grow* become fruitful   23 *As Hymen's lamps shall light you* i.e., as earnestly as you
pray that the torch of the god of marriage shall burn without smoke
(a good omen for wedded happiness)   26 *opportune* (pronounced
"oppórtune")   27 *Our worser genius can* our evil spirit can offer
29 *edge* keen enjoyment   30 *foundered* lamed   30–31 *or Phoebus'
steeds . . . below* i.e., that either day will never end or night
will never come   33 *What, Ariel* (summoning Ariel)   37 *rabble*
"thy meaner fellows"

Bestow upon the eyes of this young couple   40
Some vanity of° mine art. It is my promise,
And they expect it from me.

Ariel.   Presently?

Prospero. Ay, with a twink.

Ariel. Before you can say "Come" and "Go,"
And breathe twice and cry, "So, so,"   45
Each one, tripping on his toe,
Will be here with mop and mow.°
Do you love me, master? No?

Prospero. Dearly, my delicate Ariel. Do not approach
Till thou dost hear me call.

Ariel.   Well; I conceive.°   *Exit.*   50

Prospero. Look thou be true.° Do not give dalliance
Too much the rein; the strongest oaths are straw
To th' fire i' th' blood. Be more abstemious,
Or else good night your vow!

Ferdinand.   I warrant you, sir.
The white cold virgin snow upon my heart°   55
Abates the ardor of my liver.°

Prospero.   Well.
Now come, my Ariel; bring a corollary°
Rather than want a spirit. Appear, and pertly!
No tongue! All eyes! Be silent.   *Soft music.*

Enter Iris.°

Iris. Ceres, most bounteous lady, thy rich leas°   60
Of wheat, rye, barley, fetches,° oats, and peas;

---

41 *vanity of* illusion conjured up by   47 *mop and mow* gestures and
grimaces   50 *conceive* understand   51 *be true* (Prospero appears
to have caught the lovers in an embrace)   55 *The white cold . . .
heart* her pure white breast on mine (?)   56 *liver* (supposed seat
of sexual passion)   57 *corollary* surplus (of spirits)   59 s.d. *Iris*
goddess of the rainbow and Juno's messenger   60 *leas* meadows
61 *fetches* vetch (a kind of forage)

Thy turfy mountains, where live nibbling sheep,
And flat meads thatched with stover,° them to
    keep;
Thy banks with pionèd and twillèd brims,°
65   Which spongy April at thy hest betrims
To make cold nymphs chaste crowns; and thy
    broom groves,
Whose shadow the dismissèd bachelor loves,
Being lasslorn; thy pole-clipt vineyard;°
And thy sea-marge, sterile and rocky-hard,
70   Where thou thyself dost air°——the queen o' th'
    sky,°
Whose wat'ry arch and messenger am I,
Bids thee leave these, and with her sovereign grace,

Juno descends.°

Here on this grass plot, in this very place,
To come and sport; her peacocks fly amain.°
75   Approach, rich Ceres, her to entertain.

Enter Ceres.

Ceres. Hail, many-colored messenger, that ne'er
Dost disobey the wife of Jupiter,
Who, with thy saffron wings, upon my flow'rs
Diffusest honey drops, refreshing show'rs,
80   And with each end of thy blue bow dost crown
My bosky° acres and my unshrubbed down,
Rich scarf to my proud earth. Why hath thy queen
Summoned me hither to this short-grassed green?

Iris. A contract of true love to celebrate

63 *meads thatched with stover* (meadows covered with a kind of
grass used for winter fodder)   64 *pionèd and twillèd brims* (ob-
scure; may refer to the trenched and ridged edges of banks that
have been repaired after the erosions of winter)   68 *pole-clipt
vineyard* i.e., vineyard whose vines grow neatly around (embrace)
poles (though possibly the word is "poll-clipped," i.e., pruned)
70 *air* take the air   70 *queen o' th' sky* Juno   72 s.d. (this direction seems to come too soon, but the machine may have lowered
her very slowly)   74 *amain* swiftly (peacocks, sacred to Juno, drew
her chariot)   81 *bosky* shrubbed

And some donation freely to estate°   85
On the blessed lovers, *sexual love — not wanted now*

Ceres.   Tell me, heavenly bow,
If Venus or her son, as thou dost know,
Do now attend the Queen? Since they did plot
The means that dusky Dis my daughter got,°
Her and her blind boy's scandaled° company   90
I have forsworn.

Iris.   Of her society
Be not afraid; I met her Deity
Cutting the clouds towards Paphos,° and her son
Dove-drawn with her. Here thought they to have
     done
Some wanton charm upon this man and maid,   95
Whose vows are, that no bed-right shall be paid
Till Hymen's torch be lighted. But in vain;
Mars's hot minion is returned again;°
Her waspish-headed son° has broke his arrows,
Swears he will shoot no more, but play with
     sparrows   100
And be a boy right out.°

[*Juno alights.*]

Ceres.   Highest queen of state,
Great Juno, comes; I know her by her gait.

Juno. How does my bounteous sister? Go with me
To bless this twain, that they may prosperous be
And honored in their issue.   105

They sing.

Juno.   Honor, riches, marriage blessing,

85 *estate* bestow 89 *dusky Dis my daughter got* (alluding to the abduction of Proserpine by Pluto [Dis], god of the underworld) 90 *scandaled* scandalous 93 *Paphos* (in Cyprus, center of Venus' cult) 98 *Mars's hot minion is returned again* i.e., Mars's lustful mistress (Venus) is on her way back to Paphos 99 *waspish-headed son* (Cupid is irritable and stings with his arrows) 101 *a boy right out* an ordinary boy

many in harmony with natural

Long continuance, and increasing,
Hourly joys be still° upon you!
Juno sings her blessings on you.

110 [Ceres.]   Earth's increase, foison° plenty,
Barns and garners never empty,
Vines with clust'ring bunches growing,
Plants with goodly burden bowing;
Spring come to you at the farthest
115   In the very end of harvest.°
Scarcity and want shall shun you,
Ceres' blessing so is on you.

Ferdinand. This is a most majestic vision, and
Harmonious charmingly. May I be bold
To think these spirits?

120 *Prospero.*   Spirits, which by mine art
I have from their confines called to enact
My present fancies.

Ferdinand.   Let me live here ever!
So rare a wond'red° father and a wise
Makes this place Paradise.

Juno and Ceres whisper, and send Iris on employment.

Prospero.   Sweet now, silence!
125 Juno and Ceres whisper seriously.
There's something else to do. Hush and be mute,
Or else our spell is marred.

Iris. You nymphs, called Naiades, of the windring°
brooks,
With your sedged crowns and ever-harmless looks,
130 Leave your crisp° channels, and on this green land
Answer your summons; Juno does command.
Come, temperate nymphs, and help to celebrate
A contract of true love; be not too late.

108 *still* ever   110 *foison* abundance   114–15 *Spring come to you
. . . harvest* i.e., may there be no winter in your lives   123 *wond'red*
possessed of wonders; i.e., both wonderful and wonder-working,
and therefore to be wondered at   128 *windring* winding and wan-
dering (?)   130 *crisp* rippling

Enter certain Nymphs.

You sunburned sicklemen, of August weary,
Come hither from the furrow and be merry. 135
Make holiday; your rye-straw hats put on,
And these fresh nymphs encounter everyone
In country footing.°

*Enter certain Reapers, properly habited. They
join with the Nymphs in a graceful dance; towards the end whereof Prospero starts suddenly and speaks;° after which, to a strange,
hollow, and confused noise, they heavily°
vanish.*

*harmony
of heart
Interrupted
CALIBAN*

Prospero. [*Aside*] I had forgot that foul conspiracy
Of the beast Caliban and his confederates 140
Against my life. The minute of their plot
Is almost come. [*To the Spirits*] Well done!
Avoid!° No more!

Ferdinand. This is strange. Your father's in some
passion
That works him strongly.

Miranda.   Never till this day
Saw I him touched with anger so distempered.° 145

Prospero. You do look, my son, in a movèd sort,°
As if you were dismayed; be cheerful, sir.
Our revels now are ended. These our actors,
As I foretold you, were all spirits and
Are melted into air, into thin air; 150
And, like the baseless fabric of this vision,
The cloud-capped towers, the gorgeous palaces,
The solemn temples, the great globe itself,
Yea, all which it inherit,° shall dissolve,

→ MACBETH

138 *footing* dance   138 s.d. *speaks* (breaking the spell, which depends on silence)   138 s.d. *heavily* reluctantly   142 *Avoid* be gone
145 *distempered* violent   146 *movèd sort* troubled state   154 *it
inherit* occupy it

155 And, like this insubstantial pageant faded,
Leave not a rack° behind. We are such stuff
As dreams are made on, and our little life
Is rounded with a sleep. Sir, I am vexed.
Bear with my weakness; my old brain is troubled.
160 Be not disturbed with my infirmity.
If you be pleased, retire into my cell
And there repose. A turn or two I'll walk
To still my beating mind.

Ferdinand, Miranda.   We wish your peace.
                              Exit [*Ferdinand with Miranda*].

Prospero. Come with a thought! I thank thee, Ariel.°
Come.

Enter Ariel.

Ariel. Thy thoughts I cleave to. What's thy pleasure?

165 *Prospero.*   Spirit,
We must prepare to meet with Caliban.

Ariel. Ay, my commander. When I presented° Ceres,
I thought to have told thee of it, but I feared
Lest I might anger thee.

Prospero. Say again, where didst thou leave these
170   varlets?°

Ariel. I told you, sir, they were red-hot with drinking;
So full of valor that they smote the air
For breathing in their faces, beat the ground
For kissing of their feet; yet always bending°
175 Towards their project. Then I beat my tabor;
At which like unbacked° colts they pricked their
          ears,
Advanced° their eyelids, lifted up their noses
As they smelt music. So I charmed their ears

156 *rack* wisp of cloud   164 *I thank thee, Ariel* (for the masque?)
167 *presented* acted the part of (?) introduced (?)   170 *varlets*
ruffians   174 *bending* directing their steps   176 *unbacked* unbroken
177 *Advanced* lifted up

That calflike they my lowing followed through
Toothed briers, sharp furzes, pricking goss,° and
   thorns,   *180*
Which ent'red their frail shins. At last I left them
I' th' filthy mantled° pool beyond your cell,
There dancing up to th' chins, that the foul lake
O'erstunk their feet.

Prospero.   This was well done, my bird.
Thy shape invisible retain thou still.   *185*
The trumpery° in my house, go bring it hither
For stale° to catch these thieves.

Ariel.   I go, I go.   *Exit.*

Prospero. A devil, a born devil, on whose nature
Nurture can never stick; on whom my pains,
Humanely taken, all, all lost, quite lost!   *190*
And as with age his body uglier grows,
So his mind cankers. I will plague them all,
Even to roaring.

    Enter Ariel, loaden with glistering apparel, etc.

              Come, hang them on this line.°

   *[Prospero and Ariel remain, invisible.] Enter
     Caliban, Stephano, and Trinculo, all wet.*

Caliban. Pray you tread softly, that the blind mole
   may not
Hear a foot fall. We now are near his cell.   *195*

Stephano. Monster, your fairy, which you say is a
   harmless fairy, has done little better than played
   the Jack° with us.

Trinculo. Monster, I do smell all horse piss, at which
   my nose is in great indignation.   *200*

180 *goss* gorse   182 *filthy mantled* covered with filthy scum   186
trumpery (the "glistering apparel" mentioned in the next stage
direction)   187 *stale* decoy   193 *line* lime tree (linden)   198
Jack (1) knave (2) jack-o'-lantern, will-o'-the-wisp

Stephano. So is mine. Do you hear, monster? If I
should take a displeasure against you, look you—

Trinculo. Thou wert but a lost monster.

Caliban. Good my lord, give me thy favor still.
205   Be patient, for the prize I'll bring thee to
Shall hoodwink° this mischance. Therefore speak
    softly.
All's hushed as midnight yet.

Trinculo. Ay, but to lose our bottles in the pool—

Stephano. There is not only disgrace and dishonor in
210   that, monster, but an infinite loss.

Trinculo. That's more to me than my wetting. Yet this
is your harmless fairy, monster.

Stephano. I will fetch off my bottle, though I be o'er
ears° for my labor.

215 *Caliban.* Prithee, my king, be quiet. Seest thou here?
This is the mouth o' th' cell. No noise, and enter.
Do that good mischief which may make this island
Thine own forever, and I, thy Caliban,
For aye thy footlicker.

220 *Stephano.* Give me thy hand. I do begin to have
bloody thoughts.

Trinculo. O King Stephano! O peer!° O worthy
Stephano, look what a wardrobe here is for thee!

Caliban. Let it alone, thou fool! It is but trash.

225 *Trinculo.* O, ho, monster! We know what belongs to
a frippery.° O King Stephano!

Stephano. Put off that gown, Trinculo! By this hand,
I'll have that gown!

206 *hoodwink* put out of sight   213–14 *o'er ears* i.e., over my ears
in water   222 *peer* (alluding to the song "King Stephen was and a
worthy peer;/His breeches cost him but a crown," quoted in *Othello*
II. iii)   226 *frippery* old-clothes shop; i.e., we are good judges of
castoff clothes

Trinculo. Thy Grace shall have it.

Caliban. The dropsy drown this fool! What do you
    mean   230
To dote thus on such luggage?° Let't alone,
And do the murder first. If he awake,
From toe to crown he'll fill our skins with pinches,
Make us strange stuff.

Stephano. Be you quiet, monster. Mistress line, is not   235
    this my jerkin?° [*Takes it down.*] Now is the jerkin
    under the line.° Now, jerkin, you are like to lose
    your hair and prove a bald jerkin.°

Trinculo. Do, do!° We steal by line and level,° and't
    like° your Grace.   240

Stephano. I thank thee for that jest. Here's a garment
    for't. Wit shall not go unrewarded while I am king
    of this country. "Steal by line and level" is an ex-
    cellent pass of pate.° There's another garment for't.

Trinculo. Monster, come put some lime° upon your   245
    fingers, and away with the rest.

Caliban. I will have none on't. We shall lose our time
And all be turned to barnacles,° or to apes
With foreheads villainous low.

Stephano. Monster, lay-to your fingers; help to bear   250
    this away where my hogshead of wine is, or I'll turn
    you out of my kingdom. Go to, carry this.

Trinculo. And this.

Stephano. Ay, and this.

---

231 *luggage* useless encumbrances   236 *jerkin* kind of jacket   237
under the line pun: (1) under the lime tree (2) under the equator
238 *bald jerkin* (sailors proverbially lost their hair from fevers con-
tracted while crossing the equator)   239 *Do, do* fine, fine   239 *by
line and level* by plumb line and carpenter's level; i.e., according to
rule (with pun on "line")   239–40 *and't like* if it please   244 *pass
of pate* sally of wit   245 *lime* birdlime (which is sticky; thieves have
sticky fingers)   248 *barnacles* kind of geese supposed to have developed from shellfish

> *A noise of hunters heard. Enter divers Spirits in
> shape of dogs and hounds, hunting them about,
> Prospero and Ariel setting them on.*

255 *Prospero.* Hey, Mountain, hey!

Ariel. Silver! There it goes, Silver!

Prospero. Fury, Fury! There, Tyrant, there! Hark,
hark!

> [*Caliban, Stephano, and Trinculo are driven out.*]

Go, charge my goblins that they grind their joints
With dry convulsions,° shorten up their sinews
With agèd° cramps, and more pinch-spotted make
260   them
Than pard or cat o' mountain.°

Ariel.   Hark, they roar!

Prospero. Let them be hunted soundly. At this hour
Lies at my mercy all mine enemies.
Shortly shall all my labors end, and thou
265   Shalt have the air at freedom. For a little,
Follow, and do me service.   *Exeunt.*

ACT V

Scene I. [*In front of Prospero's cell.*]

Enter Prospero in his magic robes, and Ariel.

Prospero. Now does my project gather to a head.
My charms crack not, my spirits obey, and time
Goes upright with his carriage.° How's the day?

Ariel. On the sixth hour, at which time, my lord,

259 *dry convulsions* (such as come when the joints are dry from
old age)   260 *agèd* i.e., such as old people have   261 *pard or cat
o' mountain* leopard or catamount V.i.2–3 *time/ Goes upright with
his carriage* time does not stoop under his burden (because there is
so little left to do)

You said our work should cease.

Prospero.   I did say so   5
  When first I raised the tempest. Say, my spirit,
  How fares the King and 's followers?

Ariel.   Confined together
  In the same fashion as you gave in charge,
  Just as you left them—all prisoners, sir,
  In the line grove which weather-fends° your cell.   10
  They cannot budge till your release.° The King,
  His brother, and yours abide all three distracted,
  And the remainder mourning over them,
  Brimful of sorrow and dismay; but chiefly
  Him that you termed, sir, the good old Lord
      Gonzalo.   15
  His tears runs down his beard like winter's drops
  From eaves of reeds.° Your charm so strongly
      works 'em,
  That if you now beheld them, your affections
  Would become tender.

Prospero.   Dost thou think so, spirit?

Ariel. Mine would, sir, were I human.

Prospero.   And mine shall.   20
  Hast thou, which art but air, a touch, a feeling
  Of their afflictions, and shall not myself,
  One of their kind, that relish all as sharply,
  Passion° as they, be kindlier moved than thou art?
  Though with their high wrongs I am struck to th'
      quick,   25
  Yet with my nobler reason 'gainst my fury
  Do I take part. The rarer action is
  In virtue than in vengeance. They being penitent,
  The sole drift of my purpose doth extend
  Not a frown further. Go, release them, Ariel.   30
  My charms I'll break, their senses I'll restore,
  And they shall be themselves.

10 *weather-fends* protects from the weather   11 *till your release*
until released by you   17 *eaves of reeds* i.e., a thatched roof   24
Passion (verb)

Ariel.　　　　　　　　　　　I'll fetch them, sir.

　　　　　　　　　　　　　　　　　　　　Exit.

Prospero. Ye elves of hills, brooks, standing lakes,
　　　and groves,
　　　And ye that on the sands with printless foot
35　　Do chase the ebbing Neptune, and do fly him°
　　　When he comes back; you demi-puppets that
　　　By moonshine do the green sour ringlets° make,
　　　Whereof the ewe not bites; and you whose pastime
　　　Is to make midnight mushrumps,° that rejoice
40　　To hear the solemn curfew; by whose aid
　　　(Weak masters° though ye be) I have bedimmed
　　　The noontide sun, called forth the mutinous winds,
　　　And 'twixt the green sea and the azured vault
　　　Set roaring war; to the dread rattling thunder
45　　Have I given fire and rifted Jove's stout oak
　　　With his own bolt; the strong-based promontory
　　　Have I made shake and by the spurs° plucked up
　　　The pine and cedar; graves at my command
　　　Have waked their sleepers, oped, and let 'em forth
50　　By my so potent art. But this rough magic
　　　I here abjure; and when I have required°
　　　Some heavenly music (which even now I do)
　　　To work mine end upon their senses that°
　　　This airy charm is for, I'll break my staff,
55　　Bury it certain fathoms in the earth,
　　　And deeper than did ever plummet sound
　　　I'll drown my book.　　　　　　*Solemn music.*

*Here enters Ariel before; then Alonso, with a
frantic gesture, attended by Gonzalo; Sebastian
and Antonio in like manner, attended by Adrian
and Francisco. They all enter the circle which
Prospero had made, and there stand charmed;
which Prospero observing, speaks.*

35 *fly him* fly with him　37 *green sour ringlets* ("fairy rings," little
circles of rank grass supposed to be formed by the dancing of fairies)
39 *mushrumps* mushrooms　41 *masters* masters of supernatural
power　47 *spurs* roots　51 *required* asked for　53 *their senses that*
the senses of those whom

A solemn air, and° the best comforter
To an unsettled fancy, cure thy brains,
Now useless, boiled within thy skull! There stand,   *60*
For you are spell-stopped.
Holy Gonzalo, honorable man,
Mine eyes, ev'n sociable to the show of thine,
Fall fellowly drops.° The charm dissolves apace;
And as the morning steals upon the night,   *65*
Melting the darkness, so their rising senses
Begin to chase the ignorant fumes that mantle
Their clearer reason. O good Gonzalo,
My true preserver, and a loyal sir
To him thou follow'st, I will pay thy graces   *70*
Home° both in word and deed. Most cruelly
Didst thou, Alonso, use me and my daughter.
Thy brother was a furtherer in the act.
Thou art pinched for't now, Sebastian. Flesh and
    blood,
You, brother mine, that entertained ambition,   *75*
Expelled remorse° and nature;° whom, with
    Sebastian
(Whose inward pinches therefore are most strong),
Would here have killed your king, I do forgive thee,
Unnatural though thou art. Their understanding
Begins to swell, and the approaching tide   *80*
Will shortly fill the reasonable shore,
That now lies foul and muddy. Not one of them
That yet looks on me or would know me. Ariel,
Fetch me the hat and rapier in my cell.
I will discase° me, and myself present   *85*
As I was sometime Milan. Quickly, spirit!
Thou shalt ere long be free.
                    [*Exit Ariel and returns immediately.*]

Ariel sings and helps to attire him.

58 *and* which is   63–64 *sociable to the show . . . drops* associating
themselves with the (tearful) appearance of your eyes, shed tears
in sympathy   70–71 *pay thy graces/ Home* repay thy favors
thoroughly   76 *remorse* pity   76 *nature* natural feeling   85 *discase*
disrobe

Where the bee sucks, there suck I;
In a cowslip's bell I lie;
90 There I couch when owls do cry.
On the bat's back I do fly
After summer merrily.
Merrily, merrily shall I live now
Under the blossom that hangs on the bough.

Prospero. Why, that's my dainty Ariel! I shall miss
95   thee,
But yet thou shalt have freedom; so, so, so.
To the King's ship, invisible as thou art!
There shalt thou find the mariners asleep
Under the hatches. The master and the boatswain
100 Being awake, enforce them to this place,
And presently,° I prithee.

Ariel. I drink the air before me, and return
Or ere your pulse twice beat.   *Exit.*

Gonzalo. All torment, trouble, wonder, and amaze-
        ment
105 Inhabits here. Some heavenly power guide us
Out of this fearful country!

Prospero.   Behold, sir King,
The wrongèd Duke of Milan, Prospero.
For more assurance that a living prince
Does now speak to thee, I embrace thy body,
110 And to thee and thy company I bid
A hearty welcome.

Alonso.   Whe'r° thou be'st he or no,
Or some enchanted trifle° to abuse me,
As late I have been, I not know. Thy pulse
Beats, as of flesh and blood; and, since I saw thee,
115 Th' affliction of my mind amends, with which,
I fear, a madness held me. This must crave°
(And if this be at all)° a most strange story.
Thy dukedom I resign and do entreat

101 *presently* immediately   111 *Whe'r* whether   112 *trifle* apparition   116 *crave* require (to account for it)   117 *And if this be at
all* if this is really happening

Thou pardon me my wrongs. But how should
    Prospero
Be living and be here?

Prospero.   First, noble friend,   *120*
    Let me embrace thine age, whose honor cannot
    Be measured or confined.

Gonzalo.   Whether this be
    Or be not, I'll not swear.

Prospero.   You do yet taste
    Some subtleties° o' th' isle, that will not let you
    Believe things certain. Welcome, my friends all.   *125*
    [*Aside to Sebastian and Antonio*] But you, my
        brace of lords, were I so minded,
    I here could pluck his Highness' frown upon you,
    And justify° you traitors. At this time
    I will tell no tales.

Sebastian.   [*Aside*] The devil speaks in him.

Prospero.   No.
    For you, most wicked sir, whom to call brother   *130*
    Would even infect my mouth, I do forgive
    Thy rankest fault—all of them; and require
    My dukedom of thee, which perforce I know
    Thou must restore.

Alonso.   If thou beest Prospero,
    Give us particulars of thy preservation;   *135*
    How thou hast met us here, whom three hours
        since
    Were wracked upon this shore; where I have lost
    (How sharp the point of this remembrance is!)
    My dear son Ferdinand.

Prospero.   I am woe° for't, sir.

Alonso. Irreparable is the loss, and patience   *140*
    Says it is past her cure.

124 *subtleties* deceptions (referring to pastries made to look like
something else—e.g., castles made out of sugar)   128 *justify* prove
139 *woe* sorry

Prospero.   I rather think
You have not sought her help, of whose soft grace
For the like loss I have her sovereign aid
And rest myself content.

Alonso.   You the like loss?

145 *Prospero.* As great to me, as late,° and supportable°
To make the dear° loss, have I means much weaker
Than you may call to comfort you; for I
Have lost my daughter.

Alonso.   A daughter?
O heavens, that they were living both in Naples,
150 The King and Queen there! That they were, I wish
Myself were mudded in that oozy bed
Where my son lies. When did you lose your
      daughter?

Prospero. In this last tempest. I perceive these lords
At this encounter do so much admire°
155 That they devour their reason, and scarce think
Their eyes do offices° of truth, their words
Are natural breath. But, howsoev'r you have
Been justled from your senses, know for certain
That I am Prospero, and that very duke
160 Which was thrust forth of Milan, who most strangely
Upon this shore, where you were wracked, was
      landed
To be the lord on't. No more yet of this;
For 'tis a chronicle of day by day,
Not a relation for a breakfast, nor
165 Befitting this first meeting. Welcome, sir;
This cell's my court. Here have I few attendants,
And subjects none abroad.° Pray you look in.
My dukedom since you have given me again,
I will requite you with as good a thing,
170 At least bring forth a wonder to content ye

---

145 *As great to me, as late* as great to me as your loss, and as recent
145 *supportable* (pronounced "súpportable")   146 *dear* (intensifies the meaning of the noun)   154 *admire* wonder   156 *do offices*
perform services   167 *abroad* i.e., on the island

As much as me my dukedom.

Here Prospero discovers° Ferdinand and Miranda playing at chess.

Miranda. Sweet lord, you play me false.

Ferdinand.   No, my dearest love,
I would not for the world.

Miranda. Yes, for a score of kingdoms you should
     wrangle,
And I would call it fair play.°

Alonso.   If this prove   *175*
A vision of the island, one dear son
Shall I twice lose.

Sebastian.   A most high miracle!

Ferdinand. Though the seas threaten, they are merciful.
I have cursed them without cause.   [*Kneels.*]

Alonso.   Now all the blessings
Of a glad father compass thee about!   *180*
Arise, and say how thou cam'st here.

Miranda.   O, wonder!
How many goodly creatures are there here!
How beauteous mankind is! O brave new world
That has such people in't!

Prospero.   'Tis new to thee.

Alonso. What is this maid with whom thou wast at
     play?   *185*
Your eld'st° acquaintance cannot be three hours.
Is she the goddess that hath severed us
And brought us thus together?

Ferdinand.   Sir, she is mortal;

171 s.d. *discovers* reveals (by opening a curtain at the back of the stage)   174–75 *for a score of kingdoms . . . play* i.e., if we were playing for stakes just short of the world, you would protest as now; but then, the issue being important, I would call it fair play so much do I love you (?)   186 *eld'st* longest

But by immortal providence she's mine.
190 I chose her when I could not ask my father
For his advice, nor thought I had one. She
Is daughter to this famous Duke of Milan,
Of whom so often I have heard renown
But never saw before; of whom I have
195 Received a second life; and second father
This lady makes him to me.

Alonso.   I am hers.
But, O, how oddly will it sound that I
Must ask my child forgiveness!

Prospero.   There, sir, stop.
Let us not burden our remembrance with
A heaviness that's gone.

200 *Gonzalo.*   I have inly wept,
Or should have spoke ere this. Look down, you gods,
And on this couple drop a blessèd crown!
For it is you that have chalked forth the way
Which brought us hither.

Alonso.   I say amen, Gonzalo.

205 *Gonzalo.* Was Milan thrust from Milan that his issue
Should become kings of Naples? O, rejoice
Beyond a common joy, and set it down
With gold on lasting pillars. In one voyage
Did Claribel her husband find at Tunis,
210 And Ferdinand her brother found a wife
Where he himself was lost; Prospero his dukedom
In a poor isle; and all of us ourselves
When no man was his own.

Alonso. [*To Ferdinand and Miranda*] Give me your
hands.
Let grief and sorrow still° embrace his heart
That doth not wish you joy.

215 *Gonzalo.*   Be it so! Amen!

214 *still* forever

Enter Ariel, with the Master and Boatswain
amazedly following.

O, look, sir; look, sir! Here is more of us!
I prophesied if a gallows were on land,
This fellow could not drown. Now, blasphemy,
That swear'st grace o'erboard,° not an oath on
    shore?
Hast thou no mouth by land? What is the news?   *220*

Boatswain. The best news is that we have safely found
  Our king and company; the next, our ship,
  Which, but three glasses° since, we gave out split,
  Is tight and yare° and bravely rigged as when
  We first put out to sea.

Ariel.   [*Aside to Prospero*] Sir, all this service   *225*
  Have I done since I went.

Prospero.   [*Aside to Ariel*] My tricksy spirit!

Alonso. These are not natural events; they strengthen
  From strange to stranger. Say, how came you hither?

Boatswain. If I did think, sir, I were well awake,
  I'd strive to tell you. We were dead of sleep   *230*
  And (how we know not) all clapped under hatches;
  Where, but even now, with strange and several°
    noises
  Of roaring, shrieking, howling, jingling chains,
  And moe° diversity of sounds, all horrible,
  We were awaked; straightway at liberty;   *235*
  Where we, in all our trim, freshly beheld
  Our royal, good, and gallant ship, our master
  Cap'ring to eye° her. On a trice, so please you,
  Even in a dream, were we divided from them
  And were brought moping° hither.

Ariel. [*Aside to Prospero*]   Was't well done?   *240*

219 *That swear'st grace o'erboard* that (at sea) swearest enough to
cause grace to be withdrawn from the ship   223*glasses* hours   224
yare shipshape   232 *several* various   234 *moe* more   238 *Cap'ring*
to eye dancing to see   240 *moping* in a daze

Prospero. [*Aside to Ariel*] Bravely, my diligenc
    Thou shalt be free.

Alonso. This is as strange a maze as e'er men trod,
    And there is in this business more than nature
    Was ever conduct° of. Some oracle
    Must rectify our knowledge.

245 *Prospero.*   Sir, my liege,
    Do not infest your mind with beating on
    The strangeness of this business. At picked leisur
    Which shall be shortly, single I'll resolve you
    (Which to you shall seem probable) of every
250 These happened accidents;° till when, be cheerful
    And think of each thing well. [*Aside to Arie*
        Come hither, spirit.
    Set Caliban and his companions free.
    Untie the spell. [*Exit Ariel.*] How fares my graciou
        sir?
    There are yet missing of your company
255 Some few odd lads that you remember not.

*Enter Ariel, driving in Caliban, Stephano, and
Trinculo, in their stolen apparel.*

Stephano. Every man shift for all the rest, and let n
    man take care for himself; for all is but fortune
    Coragio,° bully-monster, *coragio!*

Trinculo. If these be true spies which I wear in m
260 head, here's a goodly sight.

Caliban. O Setebos,° these be brave spirits indeed!
    How fine my master is! I am afraid
    He will chastise me.

Sebastian.   Ha, ha!
    What things are these, my Lord Antonio?
    Will money buy 'em?

244 *conduct* conductor   248–50 *single I'll resolve . . . accident*
I myself will solve the problems (and my story will make sense t
you) concerning each and every incident that has happened   25
Coragio courage (Italian)   261 *Setebos* the god of Caliban's mothe

Antonio.   Very like. One of them   265
   Is a plain fish and no doubt marketable.

Prospero. Mark but the badges° of these men, my
     lords,
   Then say if they be true.° This misshapen knave,
   His mother was a witch, and one so strong
   That could control the moon, make flows and ebbs,   270
   And deal in her command without her power.°
   These three have robbed me, and this demi-devil
   (For he's a bastard one) had plotted with them
   To take my life. Two of these fellows you
   Must know and own; this thing of darkness I   275
   Acknowledge mine.

Caliban.   I shall be pinched to death.

Alonso. Is not this Stephano, my drunken butler?

Sebastian. He is drunk now. Where had he wine?

Alonso. And Trinculo is reeling ripe. Where should
     they
   Find this grand liquor that hath gilded 'em?   280
   How cam'st thou in this pickle?

Trinculo. I have been in such a pickle, since I saw
   you last, that I fear me will never out of my bones.
   I shall not fear flyblowing.°

Sebastian. Why, how now, Stephano?   285

Stephano. O, touch me not! I am not Stephano, but
   a cramp.

Prospero. You'd be king o' the isle, sirrah?

Stephano. I should have been a sore° one then.

Alonso. This is a strange thing as e'er I looked on.   290

267 *badges* (worn by servants to indicate to whose service they
belong; in this case, the stolen clothes are badges of their rascality)
268 *true* honest   271 *deal in her command without her power* i.e.,
dabble in the moon's realm without the moon's legitimate authority
284 *flyblowing* (pickling preserves meat from flies)   289 *sore* (1)
tyrannical (2) aching

Prospero. He is as disproportioned in his manners
    As in his shape. Go, sirrah, to my cell;
    Take with you your companions. As you look
    To have my pardon, trim it handsomely.

295 *Caliban.* Ay, that I will; and I'll be wise hereafter,
    And seek for grace. What a thrice-double ass
    Was I to take this drunkard for a god
    And worship this dull fool!

Prospero.   Go to! Away!

Alonso. Hence, and bestow your luggage where you
    found it.

300 *Sebastian.* Or stole it rather.
                [*Exeunt Caliban, Stephano, and Trinculo.*]

Prospero. Sir, I invite your Highness and your train
    To my poor cell, where you shall take your rest
    For this one night; which, part of it, I'll waste°
    With such discourse as, I not doubt, shall make it
305 Go quick away—the story of my life,
    And the particular accidents° gone by
    Since I came to this isle. And in the morn
    I'll bring you to your ship, and so to Naples,
    Where I have hope to see the nuptial
310 Of these our dear-beloved solemnizèd;°
    And thence retire me to my Milan, where
    Every third thought shall be my grave.

Alonso.   I long
    To hear the story of your life, which must
    Take° the ear strangely.

Prospero.   I'll deliver° all;
315 And promise you calm seas, auspicious gales,
    And sail so expeditious that shall catch°
    Your royal fleet far off. [*Aside to Ariel*] My Ariel,
        chick,
    That is thy charge. Then to the elements

303 *waste* spend   306 *accidents* incidents   310 *solemnizèd* (pronounced (solémnizèd")   314 *Take* captivate   314 *deliver* tell   316
catch catch up with

Be free, and fare thou well! [*To the others*] Please
you, draw near. *Exeunt omnes.*

EPILOGUE

Spoken by Prospero

Now my charms are all o'erthrown,
And what strength I have's mine own,
Which is most faint. Now 'tis true
I must be here confined by you,
Or sent to Naples. Let me not, 5
Since I have my dukedom got
And pardoned the deceiver, dwell
In this bare island by your spell;
But release me from my bands°
With the help of your good hands.° 10
Gentle breath° of yours my sails
Must fill, or else my project fails,
Which was to please. Now I want°
Spirits to enforce, art to enchant;
And my ending is despair 15
Unless I be relieved by prayer,°
Which pierces so that it assaults
Mercy itself and frees all faults.
As you from crimes would pardoned be,
Let your indulgence set me free. *Exit.* 20

FINIS

Epi. 9 *bands* bonds   10 *hands* i.e., applause to break the spell.   11
Gentle breath i.e., favorable comment   13 *want* lack   16 *prayer*
i.e., this petition

Textual Note

The Tempest was first printed in the Folio of 1623, the First Folio. The Folio text has been carefully edited and punctuated, and it has unusually complete stage directions that are probably Shakespeare's own. *The Tempest* is perhaps the finest text in the Folio, which may be why the Folio editors placed it first in the volume.

The present division into acts and scenes is that of the Folio. The present edition silently modernizes spelling and punctuation, regularizes speech prefixes, translates into English the Folio's Latin designations of act and scene, and makes certain changes in lineation in the interest either of meter, meaning, or a consistent format. Other departures from the Folio are listed below, including changes in lineation that bear upon the meaning. The reading of the present text is given first, in italics, and then the reading of the Folio (F) in roman.

The Scene: an uninhabited island . . . Names of the Actors [appears at end of play in F]

I.i.38 s.d. *Enter Sebastian, Antonio, and Gonzalo* [in F occurs after "plague," line 37]

I.ii.173 *princess'* Princesse   201 *lightnings* Lightning   271 *wast* was 282 *she* he   380 *the burden bear* beare/ the burthen

II.i.5 *master* Masters   38–39 *Antonio . . . Sebastian* [speakers reversed in F]

III.i.2 *sets* set   15 *busiest* busie lest   93 *withal* with all

III.ii.126 *scout* cout

III.iii.17 *Sebastian: I say tonight. No more* [appears in F after stage direction]   29 *islanders* Islands

IV.i.9 *off* of   13 *gift* guest   124 s.d. *Juno and....employment* [follows line 127 in F]   193 *them on* on them   231 *Let't* let's

V.i.60 *boiled* boile   72 *Didst* Did   75 *entertained* entertaine   82 *lies* ly   199 *remembrance* remembrances

The Source of "The Tempest"

There is no known source for the plot of *The Tempest*. As far as we know, *The Tempest* and *Love's Labor's Lost* are Shakespeare's two original plots. Attempts have been made to locate the source of *The Tempest* in the German comedy, *Die Schöne Sidea,* by Jakob Ayrer, who died in 1605;[1] in certain scenarios of the Italian *commedia dell' arte;*[2] in two Spanish romances.[3] The differences, however, between these plots and the plot of *The Tempest* seem more significant than the similarities. The things these plots have in common with each other and with the plot of *The Tempest* are folk-tale motifs that have long been the common property of storytellers and playwrights.[4]

If there is no source for *The Tempest,* there are documents that are relevant to it. The names of many of the characters probably derive from Thomas' *History of Italy*

[1] See H. H. Furness' Variorum Edition of *The Tempest.* Philadelphia: Lippincott, 1897, pp. 324–43, which includes a translation of Ayrer's comedy.

[2] See H. D. Gray, "The Sources of *The Tempest,*" *Modern Language Notes,* XXXV (1920), 321–30.

[3] Antonio de Eslava's *Noches de Invierno* (1609), Chap. IV. (See Hardin Craig, *Interpretation of Shakespeare.* Columbia, Missouri: Lucas Brothers, 1948, pp. 344–45. And Diego Ortuñez de Calahorra's *Espejo de Príncipes y Caballeros* (1562; English translation, 1578–1601). (See Joseph de Perott, "The Probable Source of the Plot of Shakespeare's *Tempest,*" *Publications of the Clark University Library,* I [1903–1905], 209–16.)

[4] See W. W. Newell, "Sources of Shakespeare's *Tempest,*" *Journal of American Folk-Lore,* XVI (1905), 234–57.

(1549), and the name "Setebos" derives from Robert Eden's *History of Travaile* (1577), which mentions the "great devill Setebos" worshiped by the Patagonians. Shakespeare paraphrases a passage from John Florio's translation (1603) of Montaigne's essay on the American Indians, "Of the Caniballes" (Caliban's name may derive from "cannibal"); and he paraphrases a speech of the witch, Medea, in Ovid's *Metamorphoses*—using Arthur Golding's translation (1567), which he apparently checked against the Latin original. There is good reason to believe that Shakespeare had in mind, and may even have had on his desk, when he wrote *The Tempest,* certain reports that appeared in 1610 of a tempest and a shipwreck that took place off the Bermudas in 1609. I shall print—in modernized spelling and punctuation, and with some indication of their relevance—extracts from Montaigne, Ovid, and the so-called "Bermuda pamphlets." These last require a word of explanation.

On June 2, 1609, a fleet of nine ships set sail from Plymouth for Virginia, carrying more than five hundred colonists. On July 24, a tempest off the Bermudas separated from the rest of the fleet the flagship, the *Sea-Venture,* which carried the admiral, Sir George Somers, and the new governor of the colony, Sir Thomas Gates. In the course of the next several weeks, the other ships straggled into the port at Jamestown, but the occupants of the *Sea-Venture* were given up for lost. Then, miraculously, almost a year later, on May 23, 1610, the castaways arrived in Jamestown in two small ships they had built for the journey. Their deliverance, when the news of it reached London in September, was regarded as providential. But the beneficent hand of providence emerged even more clearly when the reports of the shipwreck began to appear. For the reports showed the stormy Bermudas, which mariners had shunned as an "Ile of Divels," to be actually an island paradise.

Since Shakespeare was closely connected with the leaders of the Virginia Company (e.g., the Earls of Southampton and Pembroke) that had sponsored the expedition, he would have had good reason to read the reports of the shipwreck that appeared in 1610. The first to appear was *A Discovery of the Barmudas, otherwise called the Ile of Divels,* by Sylvester Jourdain,[5] who was with Somers. A month later there appeared *The True Declaration of the estate of the Colonie in Virginia,* which was the report of the Virginia Company.[6] Most important for our purposes is a long letter by William Strachey, who was also with Somers, which is dated July 15, 1610, but which doubtless came over to London with Gates in September. Strachey's letter was not published until 1625, in *Purchas His Pilgrimes.*[7] But it seems to have circulated in manuscript among the leaders of the Virginia Company, and we may be reasonably sure that Shakespeare read it, since it bears most closely of all the reports on *The Tempest.* It is called *A true repertory of the wracke, and redemption of Sir Thomas Gates Knight; upon, and from the Ilands of the Bermudas: his comming to Virginia, and the estate of that Colonie then, and after.*

William Strachey: from *True Repertory of the Wrack,* 1610.

[*Description of the tempest*]

A dreadful storm and hideous began to blow from out the northeast, which swelling and roaring as it were by fits, some hours with more violence than others, at length did beat all light from heaven; which like an hell of darkness turned black upon us, so much the more fuller of horror, as in such cases horror and fear use to overrun the troubled and overmastered senses of all, which (taken up with amazement) the ears lay so sensible to the terrible cries and murmurs of the winds, and distraction of our

5 Facsimile edition, ed. J. Q. Adams. New York: Scholars' Facsimiles and Reprints, 1940.

6 Reprinted in *Tracts and Other Papers,* collected by Peter Force. Washington: Force, 1844, Vol. III.

7 Glasgow: MacLehose; New York: Macmillan, 1906, Vol. XIX.

company, as who was most armed and best prepared was not a little shaken.

For four and twenty hours the storm in a restless tumult had blown so exceedingly, as we could not apprehend in our imaginations any possibility of greater violence, yet did we still find it, not only more terrible, but more constant, fury added to fury, and one storm urging a second more outrageous than the former; whether it so wrought upon our fears or indeed met with new forces. Sometimes strikes [shrieks?] in our ship amongst women and passengers not used to such hurly and discomforts made us look one upon the other with troubled hearts and panting bosoms; our clamors drowned in the winds, and the winds in thunder. Prayers might well be in the heart and lips, but drowned in the outcries of the officers. Nothing heard that could give comfort, nothing seen that might encourage hope . . . . It could not be said to rain, the waters like whole rivers did flood in the air. . . . Here the glut of water (as if throttling the wind erewhile) was no sooner a little emptied and qualified, but instantly the winds (as having gotten their mouths now free and at liberty) spake more loud and grew tumultuous and malignant. . . . There was not a moment in which the sudden splitting or instant oversetting of the ship was not expected.

Howbeit this was not all. It pleased God to bring a greater affliction yet upon us; for in the beginning of the storm we had received likewise a mighty leak. And the ship . . . was grown five foot suddenly deep with water above her ballast, and we almost drowned within whilst we sat looking when to perish from above. This, imparting no less terror than danger, ran through the whole ship with much fright and amazement, startled and turned the blood, and took down the braves of the most hardy mariner of them all, insomuch as he that before happily felt not the sorrow of others, now began to sorrow for himself when he saw such a pond of water so suddenly broken in, and which he knew could not (without present avoiding) but instantly sink him. . . .

Once, so huge a sea brake upon the poop and quarter

upon us, as it covered our ship from stern to stem, like a garment or a vast cloud, it filled her brim full for a while within, from the hatches up to the spar deck . . . . with much clamor encouraged and called upon others; who gave her now up, rent in pieces and absolutely lost. ["All lost!" . . . . "We split, we split!" I.i.52,61]

[St. Elmo's fire; Ariel: "I flamed amazement." I.ii.198]

During all this time, the heavens looked so black upon us that it was not possible the elevation of the pole might be observed; nor a star by night, not sunbeam by day was to be seen. Only upon the Thursday night, Sir George Somers, being upon the watch, had an apparition of a little round light, like a faint star, trembling, and streaming along with a sparkling blaze, half the height upon the mainmast, and shooting sometimes from shroud to shroud, tempting to settle as it were upon any of the four shrouds. And for three or four hours together, or rather more, half the night it kept with us; running sometimes along the mainyard to the very end, and then returning. At which, Sir George Somers called divers about him and showed them the same, who observed it with much wonder and carefulness. But upon a sudden, toward the morning watch, they lost the sight of it and knew not what way it made. The superstitious seamen make many constructions of this sea fire, which nevertheless is usual in storms: the same (it may be) which the Grecians were wont in the Mediterranean to call Castor and Pollux, of which, if one only appeared without the other, they took it for an evil sign of great tempest. The Italians, and such, who lie open to the Adriatic and Tyrrhene Sea, call it (a sacred Body) *Corpo sancto;* the Spaniards call it Saint Elmo, and have an authentic and miraculous legend for it. Be it what it will, we laid other foundations of safety or ruin, then in the rising or falling of it, could it have served us now miraculously to have taken our height by, it might have struck amazement, and a reverence in our devotions, according to the due of a miracle. But it did not light us any whit the more to our known way, who ran now (as do hoodwinked men) at all adventures, sometimes north, and northeast, then north and by west, and sometimes half the compass.

[*Providence*]

. . . Sir George Somers, when no man dreamed of such happiness, had discovered and cried land. . . . We were enforced to run her ashore as near the land as we could, which brought us within three-quarters of a mile of shore. . . .

We found it to be the dangerous and dreaded island, or rather islands of the Bermuda; whereof let me give your Ladyship a brief description before I proceed to my narration. And that the rather, because they be so terrible to all that ever touched on them, and such tempests, thunders, and other fearful objects are seen and heard about them, that they be called commonly the Devil's Islands, and are feared and avoided of all sea travelers alive above any other place in the world. Yet it pleased our merciful God to make even this hideous and hated place both the place of our safety and means of our deliverance.

And hereby also, I hope to deliver the world from a foul and general error: it being counted of most that they can be no habitation for men, but rather given over to devils and wicked spirits. Whereas indeed we find them now by experience to be as habitable and commodious as most countries of the same climate and situation; insomuch as if the entrance into them were as easy as the place itself is contenting, it had long ere this been inhabited as well as other islands. Thus shall we make it appear that Truth is the daughter of Time, and that men ought not to deny everything which is not subject to their own sense. [Gonzalo's speech on travelers' tales, III.iii.43–49.]

[*Caliban: "I'll not show him/ Where the quick freshes are." III.ii.70–71*]

Sure it is that there are no rivers nor running springs

of fresh water to be found upon any of them. When we came first, we digged and found certain gushings and soft bubblings which, being either in bottoms or on the side of hanging ground, were only fed with rain water which nevertheless soon sinketh into the earth and vanisheth away, or emptieth itself out of sight into the sea without any channel above or upon the superficies of the earth. For according as their rains fell, we had wells and pits (which we digged) either half full, or absolute exhausted and dry, howbeit some low bottoms (which the continual descent from the hills filled full, and in those flats could have no passage away) we found to continue as fishing ponds [Caliban: "dams . . . for fish" (?). II.ii.188], or standing pools, continually summer and winter full of fresh water.

[Caliban: "I'll get thee/ Young scamels from the rock"
(?). II.ii.179–80]

A kind of webfooted fowl there is, of the bigness of an English green plover, or seamew, which all the summer we saw not, and in the darkest nights of November and December (for in the night they only feed) they would come forth, but not fly far from home, and hovering in the air, and over the sea, made a strange hollow and harsh howling . . . which birds with a light bough in a dark night (as in our lowbelling [similar to "a-batfowling," II.i.189]) we caught. I have been at the taking of three hundred in an hour, and we might have laden our boats. Our men found a pretty way to take them, which was by standing on the rocks or sands by the seaside, and hollowing, laughing, and making the strangest outcry that possibly they could. With the noise whereof the birds would come flocking to that place, and settle upon the very arms and head of him that so cried, and still creep nearer and nearer, answering the noise themselves; by which our men would weigh them with their hand, and which weighed heaviest they took for the best and let the others alone, and so our men would take twenty dozen in two hours of the chiefest of them; and they were a good and well-relished fowl, fat and full as a partridge . . . which birds

for their blindness (for they see weakly in the day) and
for their cry and hooting, we called the sea owl.

[*Mutinies*]

In these dangers and devilish disquiets (whilst the al-
mighty God wrought for us and sent us, miraculously
delivered from the calamities of the sea, all blessings upon
the shore to content and bind us to gratefulness) thus
enraged amongst ourselves, to the destruction each of
other, into what a mischief and misery had we been given
up, had we not had a governor with his authority to have
suppressed the same? Yet was there a worse practice,
faction, and conjuration afoot, deadly and bloody, in
which the life of our governor with many others were
threatened and could not but miscarry in his fall. But such
is ever the will of God (who in the execution of His judg-
ments, breaketh the firebrands upon the head of him who
first kindleth them) there were, who conceived that our
governor indeed neither durst, nor had authority to put in
execution, or pass the act of justice upon anyone, how
treacherous or impious so ever. . . . They persevered therefore not only to draw unto them such a number and associates as they could work in to the abandoning of our
governor and to the inhabiting of this island. They had
now purposed to have made a surprise of the store-
house. . . .

But as all giddy and lawless attempts have always
something of imperfection, and that as well by the property of the action, which holdeth of disobedience and re-
bellion (both full of fear) as through the ignorance of
the devisers themselves; so in this (besides those defects)
there were some of the association, who not strong enough
fortified in their own conceits, brake from the plot itself,
and (before the time was ripe for the execution thereof)
discovered the whole order, and every agent and actor
thereof, who nevertheless were not suddenly apprehended,
by reason the confederates were divided and separated in
place, some with us, and the chief with Sir George
Somers.

*[Caliban, "on whose nature/ Nurture can never stick."
IV.i.188–89]*

[After the castaways have arrived in Virginia:] Certain Indians (watching the occasion) seized the poor fellow [one of Sir Thomas Gates's men] and led him up into the woods and sacrificed him. It did not a little trouble the lieutenant governor, who since his first landing in the country (how justly soever provoked) would not by any means be wrought to a violent proceeding against them for all the practices of villainy with which they daily endangered our men, thinking it possible by a more tractable course to win them to a better condition. But now being startled by this, he well perceived how little a fair and noble entreaty works upon a barbarous disposition, and therefore in some measure purposed to be revenged.

[Purchas has the following marginal comment: "Can a leopard change his spots? Can a savage remaining savage be civil? Were not we ourselves made and not born civil in our progenitors' days? And were not Caesar's Britons as brutish as Virginians? The Roman swords were best teachers of civility to this and other countries near us."]

Sylvester Jourdain: from *A Discovery of the Barmudas*, 1610.

[Ariel: "Safely in harbor/ Is the King's ship; in the deep nook." I.ii.226–27]

. . . All our men, being utterly spent, tired, and disabled for longer labor, were even resolved, without any hope of their lives, to shut up the hatches and to have committed themselves to the mercy of the sea (which is said to be merciless) or rather to the mercy of their mighty God and redeemer. . . . So that some of them, having some good and comfortable waters in the ship, fetched them and drunk the one to the other, taking their last leave one of the other, until their more joyful and happy meeting in a more blessed world; when it pleased God out of his most gracious and merciful providence, so to direct and guide our ship (being left to the mercy of the sea) for her most advantage; that Sir George Somers . . . most wishedly happily descried land; whereupon he most comfortably encouraged the company to follow their pumping, and by no means to cease bailing out of the water. . . . Through which weak means it pleased God to work so strongly as the water was stayed for that little time (which, as we all much feared, was the last period of our breathing) and the ship kept from present sinking, when it pleased God to send her within half an English mile of that land that Sir George Somers had not long before descried—which were the islands of the Barmudas. And there neither did our ship sink, but more fortunately in so great a misfortune fell in between two rocks, where she was fast lodged and locked for further budging.

[An island paradise]

But our delivery was not more strange in falling so opportunely and happily upon the land, as our feeding and preservation was beyond our hopes and all men's expectations most admirable. For the islands of the Barmudas, as every man knoweth that hath heard or read of them, were never inhabited by any Christian or heathen people, but ever esteemed and reputed a most prodigious and enchanted place affording nothing but gusts, storms, and foul weather; which made every navigator and mariner to avoid them, as Scylla and Charybdis, or as they would shun the Devil himself; and no man was ever heard to make for the place, but as against their wills, they have by storms and dangerousness of the rocks, lying seven leagues into the sea, suffered shipwrack. Yet did we find there the air so temperate and the country so abundantly fruitful of all fit necessaries for the sustenation and preservation of man's life, that most in a manner of all our provisions of bread, beer, and victual being quite spoiled in lying long drowned in salt water, notwithstanding we were there for the space of nine months (few days over or under) not only well refreshed, comforted, and with good satiety contented but, out of the abundance thereof, provided us some reasonable quantity and proportion of provision to carry us for Virginia and to maintain ourselves and that company we found there, to the great relief of them, as it fell out in their so great extremities . . . until it pleased God . . . that their store was better supplied. And greater and better provisions we might have had, if we had had better means for the storing and transportation thereof. Wherefore my opinion sincerely of this island is, that whereas it hath been and is full accounted the most dangerous, unfortunate, and most forlorn place of the world, it is in truth the richest, healthfulest, and pleasing land (the quantity and bigness thereof considered) and merely natural, as ever man set foot upon.

Council of Virginia: from *The True Declaration of the Estate of the Colony in Virginia,* 1610.

[*Providence*]

 . . . God that heard Jonas crying out of the belly of hell, He pitied the distresses of His servants. For behold, in the last period of necessity Sir George Somers descried land, which was by so much the more joyful by how much their danger was despairful. The islands on which they fell were the *Bermudos,* a place hardly accessible through the environing rocks and dangers. Notwithstanding, they were forced to run their ship on shore, which through God's providence fell betwixt two rocks, that caused her to stand firm and not immediately to be broken. . . .

Again, as in the great famine of Israel, God commanded Elias to fly to the brook Cedron, and there fed him by ravens; so God provided for our disconsolate people in the midst of the sea by fowls, but with an admirable difference. Unto Elias the ravens brought meat; unto our men the fowls brought themselves for meat. For when they whistled or made any strange noise, the fowls would come and sit on their shoulders; they would suffer themselves to be taken and weighed by our men, who would make choice of the fattest and fairest, and let fly the lean and lightest. . . .

Consider all these things together. At the instant of need, they descried land; half an hour more, had buried their memorial in the sea. If they had fell by night, what expectation of light from an uninhabited desert? They fell betwixt a labyrinth of rocks, which they conceive are moldered into the sea by thunder and lightning. This was not Ariadne's thread, but the direct line of God's providence. If it had not been so near land, their company or provision had perished by water; if they had not found hogs and fowls and fish, they had perished by famine; if there had not been fuel, they had perished by want of fire; if there had not been timber, they could not have transported themselves to Virginia, but must have been forgotten forever. *Nimium timet qui Deo non credit;* he is too impiously fearful that will not trust in God so powerful.

What is there in all this tragical comedy that should discourage us with impossibility of the enterprise? When of all the fleet, one only ship by a secret leak was endangered, and yet in the gulf of despair was so graciously preserved.

[*Order and disorder*]

[Disorder in Virginia:] The ground of all those miseries was the permissive providence of God, who, in the forementioned violent storm, separated the head from the body, all the vital powers of regiment being exiled with Sir Thomas Gates in those infortunate (yet fortunate) islands. The broken remainder of those supplies made a greater shipwrack in the continent of Virginia, by the tempest of dissension: every man, overvaluing his own worth, would be a commander; every man, underprizing another's value, denied to be commanded.

Michel de Montaigne: from *Of the Cannibals*, translated by John Florio, 1603.

[*Nature vs. art: Gonzalo's ideal commonwealth, II.i.148–73*]

. . . I find (as far as I have been informed) there is nothing in that nation [the American Indians], that is either barbarous or savage, unless men call that barbarism which is not common to them. As indeed, we have no other aim of truth and reason than the example and idea of the opinions and customs of the country we live in. There is ever perfect religion, perfect policy, perfect and complete use of all things. They are even savage, as we call those fruits wild which nature of herself and of her ordinary progress hath produced; whereas indeed, they are those which ourselves have altered by our artificial devices, and diverted from their common order, we should rather term savage. In those are the true and most profitable virtues and natural properties most lively and vigorous, which in these we have bastardized, applying them to the pleasure of our corrupted taste. And if notwithstanding, in divers fruits of those countries that were never tilled, we shall find that, in respect of ours, they are most excellent and as delicate unto our taste, there is no reason art should gain the point of honor of our great and puissant mother Nature. We have so much by our inventions surcharged the beauties and riches of her works that we have altogether overchoked her; yet wherever her purity shineth, she makes our vain and frivolous enterprises wonderfully ashamed. . . .

All our endeavor or wit cannot so much as reach to represent the nest of the least birdlet, its contexture, beauty, profit and use, no nor the web of a seely [i.e., trivial] spider. "All things," saith Plato, "are produced either by nature, by fortune, or by art. The greatest and fairest by one or other of the two first, the least and imperfect by the last." Those nations seem therefore so barbarous unto me, because they have received very little fashion from human wit and are yet near their original naturality. The laws of nature do yet command them, which are but little bastardized by ours, and that with such purity, as I am sometimes grieved the knowledge of it came no sooner to light, at what time there were men that better than we could have judged of it. I am sorry Lycurgus and Plato had it not; for me seemeth that what in those nations we see by experience, doth not only exceed all the pictures wherewith licentious Poesy hath proudly embellished the golden age, and all her quaint inventions to fain a happy condition of man, but also the conception and desire of Philosophy. They could not imagine a genuity so pure and simple as we see it by experience; nor ever believe our society might be maintained with so little art and humane combination. It is a nation, would I answer Plato, that hath no kind of traffic, no knowledge of letters, no intelligence of numbers, no name of magistrate, nor of politic superiority; no use of service, of riches, or of poverty; no contracts, no successions, no partitions, no occupation but idle; no respect of kindred but common, no apparel but natural, no manuring of lands, no use of wine, corn, or metal. The very words that import lying, falsehood, treason, dissimulations, covetousness, envy, detraction, and pardon, were never heard of amongst them. How dissonant would he find his imaginary commonwealth from this perfection? . . .

Furthermore, they live in a country of so exceeding pleasant and temperate situation that, as my testimonies have told me, it is very rare to see a sick body amongst them; and they have further assured me they never saw any man there either shaking with the palsy, toothless, with eyes dropping, or crooked and stooping through age.

[On cannibalism itself:] I am not sorry we note the barbarous horror of such an action, but grieved that, prying so narrowly into their faults, we are so blinded in ours. I think there is more barbarism in eating men alive than to feed upon them being dead; to mangle by tortures and torments a body full of lively sense, to roast him in pieces, to make dogs and swine to gnaw and tear him in mammocks (as we have not only read but seen very lately, yea and in our own memory, not amongst ancient enemies but our neighbors and fellow citizens; and which is worse, under pretense of piety and religion) than to roast and eat him after he is dead.

Ovid: from *Metamorphoses*, Medea's speech, translated by Arthur Golding, 1567.

[*Magic and metamorphosis: Prospero's farewell to his art V.i.33–57*]

Ye airs and winds, ye elves of hills, of brooks, of woods
    alone,
Of standing lakes, and of the night approach ye every-
    chone.
Through help of whom (the crooked banks much
    wond'ring at the thing)
I have compelled streams to run clean backward to their
    spring.
By charms I make the calm seas rough, and make the
    rough seas plain
And cover all the sky with clouds, and chase them
    thence again.
By charms I raise and lay the winds, and burst the
    viper's jaw,
And from the bowels of the earth both stones and trees
    do draw.
Whole woods and forests I remove; I make the
    mountains shake,
And even the earth itself to groan and fearfully to quake.
I call up dead men from their graves; and thee O
    lightsome Moon
I darken oft, though beaten brass abate thy peril soon.
Our sorcery dims the morning fair, and darks the sun at
    noon.

Commentaries

SAMUEL TAYLOR COLERIDGE

from *The Lectures of 1811–1812, Lecture IX*

Among the ideal plays, I will take *The Tempest,* by way of example. Various others might be mentioned, but it is impossible to go through every drama, and what I remark on *The Tempest* will apply to all Shakespeare's productions of the same class.

In this play Shakespeare has especially appealed to the imagination, and he has constructed a plot well adapted to the purpose. According to his scheme, he did not appeal to any sensuous impression (the word "sensuous" is authorized by Milton) of time and place, but to the imagination, and it is to be borne in mind that of old, and as regards mere scenery, his works may be said to have been recited rather than acted— that is to say, description and narration supplied the place of visual exhibition: the audience was told to fancy

From *Shakespearean Criticism* by Samuel Taylor Coleridge. 2nd ed., ed. Thomas Middleton Raysor. 2 vols. New York: E. P. Dutton and Company, Inc., 1960; London: J. M. Dent & Sons, Ltd., 1961. The exact text of Coleridge's lecture does not exist; what is given here is the transcript of a shorthand report taken by an auditor, J. P. Collier.

that they saw what they only heard described; the painting was not in colors, but in words.

This is particularly to be noted in the first scene—a storm and its confusion on board the king's ship. The highest and the lowest characters are brought together and with what excellence! Much of the genius of Shakespeare is displayed in these happy combinations—the highest and the lowest, the gayest and the saddest; he is not droll in one scene and melancholy in another, but often both the one and the other in the same scene. Laughter is made to swell the tear of sorrow, and to throw, as it were, a poetic light upon it, while the tear mingles tenderness with the laughter. Shakespeare has evinced the power, which above all other men he possessed, that of introducing the profoundest sentiments of wisdom, where they would be least expected, yet where they are most truly natural. One admirable secret of his art is that separate speeches frequently do not appear to have been occasioned by those which preceded, and which are consequent upon each other, but to have arisen out of the peculiar character of the speaker.

Before I go further, I may take the opportunity of explaining what is meant by mechanic and organic regularity. In the former the copy must appear as if it had come out of the same mold with the original; in the latter there is a law which all the parts obey, conforming themselves to the outward symbols and manifestations of the essential principle. If we look to the growth of trees, for instance, we shall observe that trees of the same kind vary considerably, according to the circumstances of soil, air, or position; yet we are able to decide at once whether they are oaks, elms, or poplars.

So with Shakespeare's characters: he shows us the life and principle of each being with organic regularity. The Boatswain, in the first scene of *The Tempest,* when the bonds of reverence are thrown off as a sense of danger impresses all, gives a loose to his feelings, and thus pours forth his vulgar mind to the old Counselor:

"Hence! What care these roarers for the name of King? To cabin: silence! trouble us not."

Gonzalo replies—"Good; yet remember whom thou hast aboard." To which the Boatswain answers—"None that I more love than myself. You are a counselor: if you can command these elements to silence and work the peace of the present, we will not hand a rope more; use your authority: if you cannot, give thanks that you have lived so long, and make yourself ready in your cabin for the mischance of the hour, if it so hap.— Cheerly, good hearts!—Out of our way, I say."

An ordinary dramatist would, after this speech, have represented Gonzalo as moralizing, or saying something connected with the Boatswain's language; for ordinary dramatists are not men of genius: they combine their ideas by association, or by logical affinity; but the vital writer, who makes men on the stage what they are in nature, in a moment transports himself into the very being of each personage, and, instead of cutting out artificial puppets, he brings before us the men themselves. Therefore, Gonzalo soliloquizes,—"I have great comfort from this fellow: methinks, he hath no drowning mark upon him; his complexion is perfect gallows. Stand fast, good fate, to his hanging! make the rope of his destiny our cable, for our own doth little advantage. If he be not born to be hanged, our case is miserable."

In this part of the scene we see the true sailor with his contempt of danger, and the old counselor with his high feeling, who, instead of condescending to notice the words just addressed to him, turns off, meditating with himself and drawing some comfort to his own mind by trifling with the ill expression of the Boatswain's face, founding upon it a hope of safety.

Shakespeare had predetermined to make the plot of this play such as to involve a certain number of low characters, and at the beginning he pitched the note of the whole. The first scene was meant as a lively commencement of the story; the reader is prepared for something that is to be developed, and in the next scene he brings forward Prospero and Miranda. How is this done? By giving to his favorite character, Miranda, a sentence which at once expresses the violence and fury of the storm, such as it might appear to a witness on the land, and at the same time displays the tenderness of her feelings—the exquisite feelings of a female brought up in a desert, but with all the advantages of education, all that could be communicated by a wise and affectionate father. She possesses all the delicacy of innocence, yet with all the powers of her mind unweakened by the combats of life. Miranda exclaims:

> O! I have suffered
> With those that I saw suffer: a brave vessel,
> Who had, no doubt, some noble creatures in her,
> Dash'd all to pieces.

The doubt here intimated could have occurred to no mind but to that of Miranda, who had been bred up in the island with her father and a monster only: she did not know, as others do, what sort of creatures were in a ship; others never would have introduced it as a conjecture. This shows that while Shakespeare is displaying his vast excellence, he never fails to insert some touch or other which is not merely characteristic of the particular person, but combines two things—the person, and the circumstances acting upon the person. She proceeds:

> O! the cry did knock
> Against my very heart. Poor souls! they perish'd.
> Had I been any god of power, I would
> Have sunk the sea within the earth, or e'er
> It should the good ship so have swallow'd, and
> The fraughting souls within her.

She still dwells upon that which was most wanting to the completeness of her nature—these fellow creatures from whom she appeared banished, with only one relict to keep them alive, not in her memory, but in her imagination.

Another proof of excellent judgment in the poet, for I am now principally adverting to that point, is to be found in the preparation of the reader for what is to follow. Prospero is introduced, first in his magic robe, which, with the assistance of his daughter, he lays aside, and we then know him to be a being possessed of supernatural powers. He then instructs Miranda in the story of their arrival in the island, and this is conducted in such a manner that the reader never conjectures the technical use the poet has made of the relation, by informing the auditor of what it is necessary for him to know.

The next step is the warning by Prospero that he means, for particular purposes, to lull his daughter to sleep; and here he exhibits the earliest and mildest proof of magical power. In ordinary and vulgar plays we should have had some person brought upon the stage, whom nobody knows or cares anything about, to let the audience into the secret. Prospero having cast a sleep upon his daughter, by that sleep stops the narrative at the very moment when it was necessary to break it off, in order to excite curiosity and yet to give the memory and understanding sufficient to carry on the progress of the history uninterruptedly.

Here I cannot help noticing a fine touch of Shakespeare's knowledge of human nature, and generally of the great laws of the human mind: I mean Miranda's infant remembrance. Prospero asks her—

> Canst thou remember
> A time before we came unto this cell?
> I do not think thou canst, for then thou wast not
> Out three years old.

Miranda answers,

> Certainly, sir, I can.

Prospero inquires,

> By what? by any other house or person?
> Of any thing the image tell me, that
> Hath kept with thy remembrance.

To which Miranda returns,

> 'Tis far off;
> And rather like a dream than an assurance
> That my remembrance warrants. Had I not
> Four or five women once, that tended me?

This is exquisite! In general, our remembrances of early life arise from vivid colors, especially if we have seen them in motion: for instance, persons when grown up will remember a bright green door, seen when they were quite young; but Miranda, who was somewhat older, recollected four or five women who tended her. She might know men from her father, and her remembrance of the past might be worn out by the present object, but women she only knew by herself, by the contemplation of her own figure in the fountain, and she recalled to her mind what had been. It was not that she had seen such and such grandees, or such and such peeresses, but she remembered to have seen something like the reflection of herself: it was not herself, and it brought back to her mind what she had seen most like herself.

In my opinion the picturesque power displayed by Shakespeare, of all the poets that ever lived, is only equaled, if equaled, by Milton and Dante. The presence of genius is not shown in elaborating a picture: we have had many specimens of this sort of work in modern poems, where all is so dutchified, if I may use the word, by the most minute touches, that the reader naturally asks why words, and not painting, are used? I know a young lady of much taste, who observed that in reading recent versified accounts of voyages and travels, she, by a sort of instinct, cast her eyes on the opposite page, for colored prints of what was so patiently and punctually described.

The power of poetry is, by a single word perhaps, to instill that energy into the mind which compels the imagination to produce the picture. Prospero tells Miranda,

> One midnight,
> Fated to the purpose, did Antonio open
> The gates of Milan; and i' the dead of darkness,
> The ministers for the purpose hurried thence
> Me, and thy crying self.

Here, by introducing a single happy epithet, "crying," in the last line, a complete picture is presented to the mind, and in the production of such pictures the power of genius consists.

In reference to preparation, it will be observed that the storm, and all that precedes the tale, as well as the tale itself, serve to develop completely the main character of the drama, as well as the design of Prospero. The manner in which the heroine is charmed asleep fits us for what follows, goes beyond our ordinary belief, and gradually leads us to the appearance and disclosure of a being of the most fanciful and delicate texture, like Prospero, preternaturally gifted.

In this way the entrance of Ariel, if not absolutely forethought by the reader, was foreshown by the writer: in addition, we may remark, that the moral feeling called forth by the sweet words of Miranda,

> Alack, what trouble
> Was I then to you!

in which she considered only the sufferings and sorrows of her father, puts the reader in a frame of mind to exert his imagination in favor of an object so innocent and interesting. The poet makes him wish that, if supernatural agency were to be employed, it should be used for a being so young and lovely. "The wish is father to the thought," and Ariel is introduced. Here what is called poetic faith is required and created, and our common notions of philosophy give way before it: this feeling may be said to be much stronger than historic faith, since for the exercise of poetic faith the mind is previously prepared. I make this remark, though somewhat digressive, in order to lead to a future subject of these lectures—the poems of Milton. When adverting to those, I shall have to explain farther the distinction between the two.

Many scriptural poems have been written with so much of Scripture in them that what is not Scripture appears to be not true, and like mingling lies with the most sacred revelations. Now Milton, on the other hand, has taken for his subject that one point of Scripture of which we have the mere fact recorded, and upon this he has most judiciously constructed his whole fable. So of Shakespeare's *King Lear:* we have little historic evidence to guide or confine us, and the few facts handed down to us, and admirably employed by the poet, are sufficient, while we read, to put an end to all doubt as to the credibility of the story. It is idle to say that this or that incident is improbable, because history, as far as it goes, tells us that the fact was so and so. Four or five lines in the Bible include the whole that is said of Milton's story, and the Poet has called up that poetic faith, that conviction of the mind, which is necessary to make that seem true which otherwise might have been deemed almost fabulous.

But to return to *The Tempest,* and to the wondrous creation of Ariel. If a doubt could ever be entertained whether Shakespeare was a great poet, acting upon laws arising out of his own nature and not without law, as has sometimes been idly asserted, that doubt must be removed by the character of Ariel. The very first words uttered by this being introduce the spirit, not as an angel, above man; not a gnome, or a fiend, below man; but while the poet gives him the faculties and the advantages of reason, he divests him of all mortal character, not positively, it is true, but negatively. In air he lives, from air he derives his being, in air he acts; and all his colors and properties seem to have been obtained from the rainbow and the skies. There is nothing about Ariel that cannot be conceived to exist either at sunrise or at sunset: hence all that belongs to Ariel belongs to the delight the mind is capable of receiving from the most lovely external appearances. His answers to Prospero are directly to the question and nothing beyond; or where he expatiates, which is not unfrequently, it is to himself and upon his own delights, or upon the unnatural situation in which he is placed, though under a kindly power and to good ends.

Shakespeare has properly made Ariel's very first speech characteristic of him. After he has described the manner in which he had raised the storm and produced its harmless consequences, we find that Ariel is discontented—that he has been freed, it is true, from a cruel confinement, but still that he is bound to obey Prospero and to execute any commands imposed upon him. We feel that such a state of bondage is almost unnatural to him, yet we see that it is delightful for him to be so employed. It is as if we were to command one of the winds in a different direction to that which nature dictates, or one of the waves, now rising and now sinking, to recede before it bursts upon the shore: such is the feeling we experience, when we learn that a being like Ariel is commanded to fulfill any mortal behest.

When, however, Shakespeare contrasts the treatment of Ariel by Prospero with that of Sycorax, we are sensible that the liberated spirit ought to be grateful, and Ariel does feel and acknowledge the obligation; he immediately assumes the airy being, with a mind so elastically correspondent that when once a feeling has passed from it, not a trace is left behind.

Is there anything in nature from which Shakespeare caught the idea of this delicate and delightful being, with such childlike simplicity, yet with such preternatural powers? He is neither born of heaven, nor of earth; but, as it were, between both, like a May blossom kept suspended in air by the fanning breeze, which prevents it from falling to the ground, and only finally, and by compulsion, touching earth. This reluctance of the sylph to be under the command even of Prospero is kept up through the whole play, and in the exercise of his admirable judgment Shakespeare has availed himself of it in order to give Ariel an interest in the event, looking forward to that moment when he was to gain his last and only reward—simple and eternal liberty.

Another instance of admirable judgment and excellent preparation is to be found in the creature contrasted with Ariel—Caliban, who is described in such a manner by Prospero as to lead us to expect the appearance of a foul, unnatural monster. He is not seen at once: his voice is heard; this is the preparation; he was too offensive to be seen first in all his deformity, and in nature we do not receive so much disgust from sound as from sight. After we have heard Caliban's voice he does not enter until Ariel has entered like a water nymph. All the strength of contrast is thus acquired without any of the shock of abruptness, or of that unpleasant sensation, which we experience when the object presented is in any way hateful to our vision.

The character of Caliban is wonderfully conceived: he is a sort of creature of the earth, as Ariel is a sort of creature of the air. He partakes of the qualities of the brute, but is distinguished from brutes in two ways: by having mere understanding without moral reason; and by not possessing the instincts which pertain to absolute animals. Still, Caliban is in some respects a noble being: the poet has raised him far above contempt: he is a man in the sense of the imagination: all the images he uses are drawn from nature and are highly poetical; they fit in with the images of Ariel. Caliban gives us images from the earth, Ariel images from the air. Caliban talks of the difficulty of finding fresh water, of the situation of morasses, and of other circumstances which even brute instinct, without reason, could comprehend. No mean figure is employed, no mean passion displayed, beyond animal passion and repugnance to command.

The manner in which the lovers are introduced is equally wonderful, and it is the last point I shall now mention in reference to this, almost miraculous, drama. The same judgment is observable in every scene, still preparing, still inviting, and still gratifying, like a finished piece of music. I have omitted to notice one thing, and you must give me leave to advert to it before I proceed: I mean the conspiracy against the life of Alonzo. I want to show you how well the poet prepares the feelings of the reader for this plot, which was to execute the most detestable of all crimes, and which, in another play, Shakespeare has called "the murder of sleep."

Antonio and Sebastian at first had no such intention: it was suggested by the magical sleep cast on Alonzo and Gonzalo; but they are previously introduced scoffing and scorning at what was said by others, without regard to age or situation—without any sense of admiration for the excellent truths they heard delivered, but giving themselves up entirely to the malignant and unsocial feeling which induced them to listen to everything that was said, not for the sake of profiting by the learning and experience of others, but of hearing something that might gratify vanity and self-love, by making them believe that the person speaking was inferior to themselves.

This, let me remark, is one of the grand characteristics of a villain; and it would not be so much a presentiment as an anticipation of hell for men to suppose that all mankind were as wicked as themselves, or might be so, if they were not too great fools. Pope, you are perhaps aware, objected to this conspiracy; but in my mind, if it could be omitted, the play would lose a charm which nothing could supply.

Many, indeed innumerable, beautiful passages might be quoted from this play, independently of the astonishing scheme of its construction. Everybody will call to mind the grandeur of the language of Prospero in that divine speech, where he takes leave of his magic art; and were I to indulge myself by repetitions of the kind, I should descend from the character of a lecturer to that of a mere reciter. Before I terminate, I may particularly recall one short passage which has fallen under the very severe, but inconsiderate, censure of Pope and Arbuthnot, who pronounce it a piece of the grossest bombast. Prospero thus addresses his daughter, directing her attention to Ferdinand:

The fringed curtains of thine eye advance,
And say what thou seest yond.

Taking these words as a periphrase of—"Look what is coming yonder," it certainly may to some appear to border on the ridiculous and to fall under the rule I formerly laid down—that whatever, without injury, can be translated into a foreign language in simple terms, ought to be in simple terms in the original language; but it is to be borne in mind that different modes of expression frequently arise from difference of situation and education: a blackguard would use very different words, to express the same thing, to those a gentleman would employ, yet both would be natural and proper; difference of feeling gives rise to difference of language: a gentleman speaks in polished terms, with due regard to his own rank and position, while a blackguard, a person little better than half a brute, speaks like half a brute, showing no respect for himself nor for others.

But I am content to try the lines I have just quoted by the introduction to them; and then, I think, you will admit, that nothing could be more fit and appropriate than such language. How does Prospero introduce them? He has just told Miranda a wonderful story, which deeply affected her and filled her with surprise and astonishment, and for his own purposes he afterwards lulls her to sleep. When she awakes, Shakespeare has made her wholly inattentive to the present, but wrapped up in the past. An actress who understands the character of Miranda would have her eyes cast down and her eyelids almost covering them, while she was, as it were, living in her dream. At this moment Prospero sees Ferdinand and wishes to point him out to his daughter, not only with great, but with scenic solemnity, he standing before her and before the spectator in the dignified character of a great magician. Something was to appear to Miranda on the sudden, and as unexpectedly as if the hero of a drama were to be on the stage at the instant when the curtain is elevated. It is under such circumstances that

Prospero says, in a tone calculated at once to arouse his daughter's attention,

> The fringed curtains of thine eye advance,
> And say what thou seest yond.

Turning from the sight of Ferdinand to his thoughtful daughter, his attention was first struck by the downcast appearance of her eyes and eyelids; and, in my humble opinion, the solemnity of the phraseology assigned to Prospero is completely in character, recollecting his pre-ternatural capacity, in which the most familiar objects in nature present themselves in a mysterious point of view. It is much easier to find fault with a writer by reference to former notions and experience than to sit down and read him, recollecting his purpose, connecting one feeling with another, and judging of his words and phrases in pro-portion as they convey the sentiments of the persons represented.

Of Miranda we may say that she possesses in herself all the ideal beauties that could be imagined by the great-est poet of any age or country; but it is not my purpose now so much to point out the high poetic powers of Shakespeare as to illustrate his exquisite judgment, and it is solely with this design that I have noticed a passage with which, it seems to me, some critics, and those among the best, have been unreasonably dissatisfied. If Shake-speare be the wonder of the ignorant, he is, and ought to be, much more the wonder of the learned: not only from profundity of thought, but from his astonishing and in-tuitive knowledge of what man must be at all times and under all circumstances, he is rather to be looked upon as a prophet than as a poet. Yet, with all these unbounded powers, with all this might and majesty of genius, he makes us feel as if he were unconscious of himself and of his high destiny, disguising the half god in the sim-plicity of a child.

E. M. W. TILLYARD

The Tragic Pattern: "The Tempest"

It is a common notion that *Cymbeline* and *The Winter's Tale* are experiments leading to the final success of *The Tempest*. I think it quite untrue of *The Winter's Tale*, which, in some ways though not in others, deals with the tragic pattern more adequately than the later play. Certainly it deals with the destructive portion more directly and fully. On the other hand, *The Tempest*, by keeping this destructive portion largely in the background and dealing mainly with regeneration, avoids the juxtaposition of the two themes, which some people (of whom I am not one) find awkward in *The Winter's Tale*. The simple truth is that if you cram a trilogy into a single play something has to be sacrificed. Shakespeare chose to make a different sacrifice in each of his two successful renderings of the complete tragic pattern: unity in *The Winter's Tale*, present rendering of the destructive part of the tragic pattern in *The Tempest*.

Many readers, drugged by the heavy enchantments of Prospero's island, may demur at my admitting the tragic

From *Shakespeare's Last Plays* by E. M. W. Tillyard. London: Chatto and Windus, Ltd., 1938. Reprinted by permission of Chatto and Windus, Ltd., and Barnes and Noble, Inc.

element to the play at all. I can cite in support one of the
latest studies of the play, Dover Wilson's[1] (although I
differ somewhat in the way I think the tragic element is
worked out). Of the storm scene he writes:

> It is as if Shakespeare had packed his whole tragic vision
> of life into one brief scene before bestowing his new vision
> upon us.

But one has only to look at the total plot to see that in
its main lines it closely follows those of *Cymbeline* and
The Winter's Tale, and that tragedy is an organic part of
it. Prospero, when one first hears of him, was the ruler of
an independent state and beloved of his subjects. But
all is not well, because the King of Naples is his enemy.
Like Basilius in Sidney's *Arcadia,* he commits the error
of not attending carefully enough to affairs of state. The
reason for this error, his Aristotelian ἀμαρτία, is his love
of study. He hands over the government to his brother
Antonio, who proceeds to call in the King of Naples to
turn Prospero out of his kingdom. Fearing the people,
Antonio refrains from murdering Prospero and his infant
daughter, but sets them adrift in a boat. Now, except
for this last item, the plot is entirely typical of Elizabethan
revenge tragedy. Allow Prospero to be put to death, give
him a son instead of a daughter to live and to avenge
him, and your tragic plot is complete. Such are the affini-
ties of the actual plot of *The Tempest*. And in the abstract it is more typically tragic in the fashion of its age
than *The Winter's Tale*, with its debt to the Greek
romances.

In handling the theme of regeneration, Shakespeare
in one way alters his method. Although a royal person
had previously been the protagonist, it had been only in
name. Cymbeline had indeed resembled Prospero in having his enemies at his mercy and in forgiving them, but
he owed his power not to himself, but to fortune and

1 *The Meaning of the Tempest,* the Robert Spence Watson Memorial
Lecture for 1936, delivered before the Literary and Philosophical Society
of Newcastle-upon-Tyne, on October 5th, 1936.

the efforts of others. As for Leontes, he has little to do
with his own regeneration; for it would be perverse to
make too much of his generosity in sheltering Florizel
and Perdita from the anger of Polixenes. But Prospero
is the agent of his own regeneration, the parent and tutor
of Miranda; and through her and through his own works
he changes the minds of his enemies. It was by this cen-
tering of motives in Prospero as well as by subordinating
the theme of destruction that Shakespeare gave *The Tempest* its unified structure.

In executing his work, Shakespeare chose a method
new to himself but repeated by Milton in *Samson Agonis-
tes*. He began his action at a point in the story so late
that the story was virtually over; and he included the
total story either by narrating the past or by re-enacting
samples of it: a complete reaction from the method of
frontal attack used in *The Winter's Tale*.

For the re-enactment of tragedy it is possible to think
with Dover Wilson that the storm scene does this. But
it does nothing to re-enact the specific tragic plot in the
play, the fall of Prospero; and one of its aims is to sketch
(as it does with incomparable swiftness) the characters
of the ship's company. The true re-enactment is in the
long first scene of the second act where Antonio, in per-
suading Sebastian to murder Alonso, personates his own
earlier action in plotting against Prospero, thus drawing
it out of the past and placing it before us in the present.
This long scene, showing the shipwrecked king and
courtiers and the conspiracy, has not had sufficient praise
nor sufficient attention. Antonio's transformation from
the cynical and lazy badgerer of Gonzalo's loquacity to
the brilliantly swift and unscrupulous man of action is
a thrilling affair. Just so Iago awakes from his churlish
"honesty" to his brilliant machinations. Antonio is indeed
one of Shakespeare's major villains:

Antonio.   Will you grant with me
   That Ferdinand is drown'd?

Sebastian.   He's gone.

Antonio.   Then, tell me,
  Who's the next heir to Naples?

Sebastian.   Claribel.

Antonio. She that is Queen of Tunis; she that dwells
  Ten leagues beyond man's life; she that from Naples
  Can have no note, unless the sun were post—
  The man i' the moon's too slow—till newborn chins
  Be rough and razorable; she that from whom
  We all were sea-swallow'd, though some cast again,
  And by that destiny, to perform an act
  Whereof what's past is prologue, what to come,
  In yours and my discharge.

Sebastian.   What stuff is this! how say you?
  'Tis true my brother's daughter's Queen of Tunis;
  So is she heir of Naples; 'twixt which regions
  There is some space.

Antonio.   A space whose every cubit
  Seems to cry out, "How shall that Claribel
  Measure us back to Naples? Keep in Tunis,
  And let Sebastian wake." Say this were death
  That now hath seized them; why, they were no worse
  Than now they are. There be that can rule Naples
  As well as he that sleeps; lords that can prate
  As amply and unnecessarily
  As this Gonzalo; I myself could make
  A chough of as deep chat. O, that you bore
  The mind that I do! What a sleep were this
  For your advancement! Do you understand me?

We should do wrong to take the conspiracy very seriously
in itself. We know Prospero's power, and when Ariel
enters and wakes the intended victims we have no fears
for their future safety. But all the more weight should the
scene assume as recalling the past.

    Dover Wilson[2] greatly contributes to a right under-
standing of the play by stressing the first lines of the fifth
act, when Prospero declares to Ariel that he will pardon
his enemies, now quite at his mercy:

2 *Op. cit.,* pp. 14–18.

Ariel.   Your charm so strongly works 'em
That if you now beheld them, your affections
Would become tender.

Prospero.   Dost thou think so, spirit?

Ariel. Mine would, sir, were I human.

Prospero.   And mine shall.
Hast thou, which art but air, a touch, a feeling
Of their afflictions, and shall not myself,
One of their kind, that relish all as sharply,
Passion as they, be kindlier moved than thou art?
Though with their high wrongs I am struck to the quick,
Yet with my nobler reason 'gainst my fury
Do I take part: the rarer action is
In virtue than in vengeance: they being penitent,
The sole drift of my purpose doth extend
Not a frown further.

But when Dover Wilson would have this to represent
Prospero's sudden conversion from a previously intended
vengeance, I cannot follow him. It is true that Prospero
shows a certain haste of temper up to that point of the
play, and that he punishes Caliban and the two other
conspirators against his life with some asperity; but his
comments on them, after his supposed conversion, have
for me the old ring:

Mark but the badges of these men, my lords,
Then say if they be true. This misshapen knave,
His mother was a witch, and one so strong
That could control the moon, make flows and ebbs,
And deal in her command without her power.
These three have robb'd me; and this demi-devil—
For he's a bastard one—had plotted with them
To take my life. Two of these fellows you
Must know and own; this thing of darkness I
Acknowledge mine.

The last words express all Prospero's old bitterness that
Caliban has resisted him and refused to respond to his

nurture.[3] Indeed, Prospero does not change fundamentally during the play, though, like Samson's, his own accomplished regeneration is put to the test. If he had seriously intended vengeance, why should he have stopped Sebastian and Antonio murdering Alonso? That he did stop them is proof of his already achieved regeneration from vengeance to mercy. This act, and his talk to Ariel of taking part with his reason against his fury, are once again a re-enactment of a process now past, perhaps extending over a period of many years. I do not wish to imply that the re-enactment is weak or that the temptation to vengeance was not there all the time. Prospero's fury at the thought of Caliban's conspiracy, which interrupts the masque, must be allowed full weight. It is not for nothing that Miranda says that—

> never till this day
> Saw I him touch'd with anger so distemper'd.

We must believe that Prospero felt thus, partly because Caliban's conspiracy typifies all the evil of the world which has so perplexed him, and partly because he is still tempted to be revenged on Alonso and Antonio. He means to pardon them, and he will pardon them. But beneath his reason's sway is this anger against them, which, like Satan's before the sun in *Paradise Lost,* disfigures his face. When Dover Wilson calls Prospero

> a terrible old man, almost as tyrannical and irascible as Lear at the opening of his play,

he makes a valuable comparison, but it should concern Prospero as he once was, not the character who meets us in the play, in whom these traits are mere survivals.

The advantage of this technique of re-enactment was economy, its drawback an inevitable blurring of the sharp outline. The theme of destruction, though exquisitely blended in the whole, is less vivid than it is in *The*

---

[3] See the admirable discussion of "nature" and "nurture" in *The Tempest* in Middleton Murry's *Shakespeare,* pp. 396 ff.

Winter's Tale. Having made it so vivid in that play, Shakespeare was probably well content to put the stress on the theme of re-creation. And here he did not work solely by re-enactment. He strengthened Prospero's re-enacted regeneration by the figures of Ferdinand and Miranda. I argued above that, in view of his background of Elizabethan chivalrous convention, Ferdinand need not have been as insignificant as he is usually supposed. Similarly, Miranda's character has been unduly diminished in recent years. Today, under the stress of the new psychology, men have become nervous lest they should be caught illicitly attaching their daydreams of the perfect woman to a character in fiction. They laugh at the Victorians for falling unawares into this error, and Miranda may have been one of the most popular victims. Hence the anxiety not to admire her too much. E. K. Chambers has written:

> Unless you are sentimentalist inveterate, your emotions will not be more than faintly stirred by the blameless loves at first sight of Ferdinand and Miranda.

Schücking[4] goes further and considers Miranda a poor imitation of Beaumont and Fletcher's idea of the chaste female, an idea that could be dwelt on so lovingly and emphatically only in a lascivious age. In depicting her with her talk of "modesty, the jewel in my dower" and her protests that if Ferdinand will not marry her, "I'll die your maid," and in making Prospero so insistent that she should not lose her maidenhead before marriage, Shakespeare, according to Schücking, is yielding to the demands of his age against his own better judgment. But Miranda is sufficiently successful a symbolic figure for it to matter little if she makes conventional and, in her, unnatural remarks. And even this defense may be superfluous. Since Miranda had never seen a young man, it might reasonably be doubted whether she would behave herself with entire propriety when she did. Prospero, too, had made enough mistakes in his life to

---

[4] *Character Problems in Shakespeare's Plays,* pp. 249–50.

be very careful to make no more. Further, Miranda was the heiress to the Duchy of Milan and her father hoped she would be Queen of Naples. What most strikingly emerged from the abdication of our late King was the strong "anthropological" feeling of the masses of the people concerning the importance of virginity in a king's consort. The Elizabethans were not less superstitious than ourselves and would have sympathized with Prospero's anxiety that the future Queen of Naples should keep her maidenhead till marriage: otherwise ill luck would be sure to follow.

To revert to Miranda's character, like Perdita she is both symbol and human being, yet in both capacities somewhat weaker. She is the symbol of "original virtue," like Perdita, and should be set against the devilish figure of Antonio. She is the complete embodiment of sympathy with the men she thinks have been drowned: and her instincts are to create, to mend the work of destruction she has witnessed. She is—again like Perdita, though less clearly—a symbol of fertility. Stephano asks of Caliban, "Is it so brave a lass?" and Caliban answers,

> Ay, lord; she will become thy bed, I warrant,
> And bring thee forth brave brood.

Even if *The Tempest* was written for some great wedding, it need not be assumed that the masque was inserted merely to fit the occasion. Like the goddesses in Perdita's speeches about the flowers, Juno and Ceres and the song they sing may be taken to reinforce the fertility symbolism embodied in Miranda:

Juno.   Honor, riches, marriage blessing,
          Long continuance, and increasing,
          Hourly joys be still upon you!
          Juno sings her blessings on you.

Ceres. Earthës increase, foison plenty,
          Barns and garners never empty,
          Vines with clustering bunches growing,

Plants with goodly burthen bowing;

Spring come to you at the farthest
In the very end of harvest!
Scarcity and want shall shun you;
Ceres' blessing so is on you.

The touches of ordinary humanity in Miranda—her siding with Ferdinand against a supposedly hostile father, for instance—are too well known to need recalling. They do not amount to a very great deal and leave her vaguer as a human being than as a symbol. Middleton Murry is not at his happiest when he says that "they are so terribly, so agonizingly real, these women of Shakespeare's last imagination." As far as Miranda is concerned, any agonizing sense of her reality derives from the critic and not from the play. But this does not mean that, judged by the play's requirements (which are not those of brilliant realism), Miranda is not perfection. Had she been more weakly drawn, she would have been insignificant, had she been more strongly, she would have interfered with the unifying dominance of Prospero.

Not only do Ferdinand and Miranda sustain Prospero in representing a new order of things that has evolved out of destruction; they also vouch for its continuation. At the end of the play Alonso and Prospero are old and worn men. A younger and happier generation is needed to secure the new state to which Prospero has so painfully brought himself, his friends, and all his enemies save Caliban.

BERNARD KNOX

"The Tempest" and the Ancient Comic Tradition

In *The Tempest* Shakespeare abandons the three familiar *milieux* in which most of his plays are set (classical antiquity, medieval England, and Renaissance Europe)[1] for a nameless island which is remote even from that Tunis which is itself, according to Antonio, "ten leagues beyond man's life." This island is not only uncharted, it is one on which anything can happen; "All torment, trouble, wonder, and amazement Inhabits heere." The poet places his characters in a world which seems to be purely of his own creating; it seems in this respect significant that, in spite of prodigies of *Quellenforschung,* no satisfactory source of *The Tempest* has yet been identified.

In the so-called "romances" of Shakespeare's last period there is an accelerated flight from probability; it is a movement beyond the "probable impossibility" to the

From *English Stage Comedy*. English Institute Essays, 1954, ed. W. K. Wimsatt, Jr. New York, Columbia University Press, 1955, pp. 52–73. Reprinted by permission of Columbia University Press.
[1] Cf. Gilbert Highet, *The Classical Tradition* (Oxford, 1949), p. 194.

complete impossibility. In *The Tempest* the laws which
govern objects existing in space and time as we know
them are imperiously suspended. Until the solemn moment when Prospero abjures his rough magic, the action
develops in a world which defies nature: "These are not
naturall events, they strengthen From strange, to stranger."
One wonders how Prospero can keep his promise to the
bewildered Alonso—"I'le resolve you (Which to you
shall seeme probable) of every These happend accidents."

A recent production by the Yale Dramatic Association
presented *The Tempest* as "science fiction"; the shipwreck
scene took place in a space ship, and the action which
takes place away from Prospero's cell was seen on a
gigantic television screen, tuned in by a Prospero who
sat before a control board which buzzed and flashed
green light. The point was well taken: Shakespeare has
in fact done what the modern science-fictioneers do—
substituted for the normal laws of the operation of matter
a new set of laws invented for the occasion.

Such a substitution creates great possibilities for what
Aristotle called "Spectacle," and if the Yale Dramatic
Association developed those possibilities somewhat ex-
uberantly along modern lines they at least did no worse
than Dryden and Davenant in 1667, whose stage direction for Act I, scene i, reads, in part: "This Tempest
. . . has many dreadful Objects in it, as several Spirits
in horrid shapes flying down among the Sailers, then
rising and crossing in the Air. And when the Ship is
sinking, the whole House is darken'd, and a shower of
Fire falls upon 'em."

But novel and fantastic effects (and in this play it is
clear that Shakespeare was interested in producing them)
have their dangerous side; they may, by trading too
much on it, destroy that willing suspension of disbelief
on which every dramatic performance depends—the audience may come to feel, with Gonzalo, "Whether this
be Or be not, I'le not sweare." The dramatist, by asking
too much, may lose everything. Such a defiance of the
normal laws of cause and effect in the operations of
nature is especially dangerous in comedy, for comedy's

appeal, no matter how contrived the plot may be, is to the audience's sense of solid values in a real world, to a critical faculty which can recognize the inappropriate. Tragedy, which questions normal human assumptions, may introduce the super- and the hypernatural more safely than comedy, which depends on the solidity of those assumptions for a response. A comic poet who sets his characters in action, not in the world as we know it but in one which defies our expectation, must compensate for the strangeness of the events by making the essences and relationships of the characters immediately and strikingly familiar. To put in another way, the fantasy and originality of the setting must be balanced and disciplined by a rigid adherence to tradition in character and plot.

This, I suggest, is a valid formula for *The Tempest*. It has certainly the most extraordinary and fantastic setting, for the sorcery of Prospero is a stranger thing than the familiar English fairy magic of *A Midsummer Night's Dream*. But in other ways it is the most rigidly traditional of all Shakespeare's comedies—with one exception. The exception is *The Comedy of Errors,* which is however apprentice work, a typical Renaissance *remaniement* of a Plautine original. *The Tempest* is as original as *The Comedy of Errors* is imitative; and yet they are the beginning and end of the same road. For the traditional foundation on which *The Tempest*'s cloud-capped towers are raised is the ancient comedy of Plautus, Terence, and (though the name would not have meant much to Shakespeare) Menander.

Like all proper foundations, this one is not conspicuous. But there are odd corners where its outline is visible in the superstructure. This, for example:

Prospero. [*To Ariel*] She did confine thee
    By helpe of her more potent Ministers,
    And in her most unmittigable rage,
    Into a cloven Pyne, within which rift,
    Imprison'd, thou didst painefully remaine
    A dozen yeeres: within which space she di'd,

And left thee there: where thou didst vent thy groanes
As fast as Mill-wheeles strike.

The groans of a disobedient spirit imprisoned in a
cloven pine by a "blew ey'd hag" come "as fast as Mill-
wheeles strike": the simile illustrates the unfamiliar by
appeal to an aspect of ordinary experience. Yet not,
presumably, Ariel's ordinary experience: there are no
mills in the strange economy of Prospero's island. The
simile illustrates by an appeal from one world to another,
with an anachronism the reverse of those Homeric sim-
iles which compare conditions of the heroic age to those
of the poet's own time. (Homer compares the voice of
Achilles to a trumpet, an instrument which the embattled
heroes of his poem never mention or use, almost certainly because it had not yet been invented.) The mill
wheels of Shakespeare's simile come not from his own
world but from the world of Plautine comedy, where
with monotonous frequency the rebellious slave is threatened or actually punished with an assignment to the
brutal labor of the mill. And in this fantastic context,
where Ariel ("my slave, as thou reportst thyselfe") is
reminded of his punishment for former disobedience and
threatened with even worse punishment for present disobedience, the simile gives a touch of familiarity and
proportion to the outlandish details of Ariel's nature and
status.

Here the classical precedent is for a moment distinctly
visible, but in general it does its work the more efficiently
because it is not obtrusive. Below the strange and brilliant surface composed of medieval magic and Renaissance travel tales, the initial situation, the nature and relationships of most of the characters, the development
of the action and its final solution are all conjugations
of the basic paradigms of classical comedy.

One of the most influential of these paradigms relates
to the existence in ancient society of a dividing line
stricter and more difficult to cross than any social bar-
rier has been since: the distinction between slave and
free. The free man could not imagine a misfortune worse

than slavery, nor the slave a greater blessing than freedom. Slave and free were not so much separate classes
as separate worlds: Aristotle could go so far as to claim
that they were separate natures. This division was the
most important sociological datum of ancient society,
affecting men's attitude toward each other with a power
almost as great as that of natural differences of sex or
color. Among other things it provided a fixed contrast
of condition and standards on which comedy could be
based.

Ancient tragedy at the height of its development ig-
nores the division and deals only with free men; Attic
tragedy did not deal with slaves until Euripides introduced them, and this innovation was one of the main
grounds for the conservative attack on him. The place
for slaves was comedy, which, says Aristotle, "is an imitation of characters of a lower type"; and the lowest type
imaginable was the slave. Comic slaves could be beaten,
could curse, lie, cheat, be drunken, lecherous, and cow-
ardly to the limit of the free audience's capacity for
laughter without offending its sense of propriety and
human dignity. Such an exhibition might in fact be considered to have a moral effect; in Plutarch's "Life of
Lycurgus" (Chap. 28) we are told that at Sparta the
ephors introduced into the military dining halls Helots
who had been deliberately inebriated as a spectacle to
teach the young what drunkenness was like; they also
made the Helots learn songs and dances that were, to
quote Plutarch again, "ignoble and ridiculous."

This was, of course, not a real dramatic performance
(though there is evidence of some kind of comic performance at Sparta from quite early times); at Athens
the picture is clearer. It is perhaps only a coincidence
that the chorus of satyrs in the only two surviving specimens of the humorous satyr play are, in the plot of the
plays, temporarily enslaved, but it is evident that typical
Athenian Old Comedy depended heavily on the laughter
to be extracted from the low proclivities and activities
of slaves. Aristophanes is not typical, but he indicates
what is typical in a famous passage of self-congratulation

which sets forth his claim to have ennobled comedy. Among other things he claims to have "liberated the slaves, whom the poets always brought on stage howling, all for the sake of the same old joke, so that a fellow slave could make fun of their stripes and ask them, 'What happened to your hide, poor devils? Were your sides assaulted by a whiplash army that cut down the trees on your back?' " Aristophanes did not, of course, dispense entirely with servile humor, rather he seems to have adapted it to subtler purposes by introducing witty contrasts between slave and free. In *The Knights,* for instance, he brings on stage all the prominent Athenian politicians of the day as slaves in the house of a bad-tempered old man called Demos: in this comedy Demosthenes' Nicias and Cleon fight, cheat, drink, spy, play the coward, curse, bawl, lie, and rant as valiantly as any slave ever born. Here the humorous aspects of servile behavior are used to make a satiric point, that the free men behave like slaves; *The Frogs* makes the opposite point by ringing the changes on the contrast between the master Dionysus and his slave Xanthias, who repeatedly exchange identities—with the surprising result that the slave emerges as his master's superior in wit, courage, and, incidentally, literary taste, for Xanthias cannot abide Euripides.

In the comedy of the fourth century the magnificent fantasy and political wit of Aristophanes are sadly lacking, but the theme of contrast between slave and free remains. In the domestic comedy of Menander and his contemporaries (the models of the Roman comic poets) the theme crystallizes into a variety of stock patterns, which have exerted enormous influence on comedy ever since.

In this comedy the master design is always more or less the same. A domestic problem involving the free members of the household (usually, in Menander, a marriage or a seduction—sometimes both) is eventually solved through complicated intrigues which involve the slave members of the household. The comedy proceeds on two social levels which interpenetrate, often on two plot levels as well, which also interpenetrate. The slave characters (and a host of technically free but hardly distinguishable lower-class types such as parasites, butlers, cooks, and pimps) have their own problems (the attainment of freedom, a free meal or a free drink), the solution of which is artfully made to depend on the solution of the problem of the free characters. A typical paradigm is the plot in which a clever slave, by intelligent initiative and intrigue (often directed against his less intelligent fellow slaves) solves his master's problem (which may range from finding a wife to marrying off a child) and, as a reward for his services, gains his private objective, his liberty.

This is a slave who has the intelligence of, and eventually attains the status of, a free man; but there is another type of slave who is a convenient vehicle for the traditional servile humor. This one provides the sullen bad temper, the cursing, the drunkenness, the indecency, thievishness, and cowardice which are the traditional characteristics of the comic slave. He may have the same ambition as his cleverer fellow, but not the same capacity; he forms grand designs, but through stupidity (often through the direct intervention of the clever slave) he fails miserably, and is humiliated and punished with blows or a stint at the mill.

While the slaves, in aspiration and action, trespass on the confines of the free world, the freeborn may find themselves, as foundlings, kidnapped children, or prisoners of war, temporary denizens of the slave world; their identification and restoration to freedom (and usually marriage) is the play's denouement, and usually coincides with, and balances, the liberation of the clever slave or the restoration of the stupid slave to his proper station, or both. Together with these contrasts of condition there are deeper contrasts of nature; free men can think and act like slaves and slaves rise superior in intelligence or emotion to their masters. One of the most searching and profound of Roman comedies is Lessing's favorite, *The Captives* of Plautus, in which master and slave, both enslaved as prisoners of war, exchange identities so that the master (as the slave) can be released to take the ransom demand home, while the slave remains in slavery (as the master), risking and, as it turns out, suffering terrible punishment when the truth is discovered. The nobility displayed by the slave is, characteristically enough, justified at the end of the play by the discovery that he was really born free, and his liberation is balanced by the punishment of the slave who originally kidnapped and sold him into slavery. In this and in practically all Roman comedy, the finale is a restoration of the characters to their proper status; in the typical pattern, the restoration of one of the two young lovers to freedom makes possible their marriage, and the stern father releases the clever and independent slave who has been instrumental in bringing about the happy conclusion.

When the dramatists of the Renaissance began to imitate the Roman comedies, slavery was a thing of the past in Europe (though not a few Elizabethan worthies made their fortunes by introducing it into the West Indies), but the ancient comic design was easily adapted to the conditions of a society which, like that of Elizabethan England, was based, however insecurely, on hierarchical social categories. Shakespearean comedy abounds in brilliant adaptations of the basic formula: the cruel reduction to his proper station suffered by Malvolio, who had "greatnesse thrust" upon him; the exposure of Parolles "the gallant militarist" as a "past-saving slave"; above all the magnificent interpenetration of the two worlds of court and tavern in *Henry IV*. Falstaff acts the role of the King in the Boar's Head, runs his sword through Hotspur's corpse at Shrewsbury, and sets out for London crying, "The Lawes of England are at my commandment," only to be brusquely restored to his proper station as a "Foole and Jester." Prince Hal, like some foundling, as his father suggests, begins as "sworn brother to a leash of Drawers," sounding "the very base-string of humility," but in the end restores himself to his proper station, "to mock the expectation of the world."

But in *The Tempest,* a Utopia which Shakespeare invented for himself (as Gonzalo invents his in the play), there is no need to translate the classic form: it can be used literally. Prospero is master (and incidentally an irritable old man with a marriageable daughter) and Ariel and Caliban are slaves. Prospero as sorcerer has the power to enslave and release the free men too: this contrast is relevant for all the characters of the play—one of its main components is what Brower has called "the slavery-freedom continuity." "The 'slaves' and 'servants' of the play," he points out, 'suffer various kinds of imprisonment, from Ariel in his 'cloven pine' to Ferdinand's mild confinement, and before the end of Act IV everyone except Prospero and Miranda has been imprisoned in one way or another. During the course of Act V all the prisoners except Ferdinand (who has already been released) are set free. . . ."[2]

After the long expository scene between Prospero and Miranda (itself a typical Plautine delayed prologue) we are presented with an interview between master and intelligent slave:

> All haile, great Master, grave Sir, haile: I come
> To answer Thy best pleasure; be't to fly,
> To swim, to dive into the fire: to ride
> On the curld clowds: to thy strong bidding, taske.
> Ariel, and all his Qualitie.

This is servile enough, and comparable to many a hyperbolic declaration of availability made by Roman comic slaves; its comic tone is pointed up by the fact that the moment Ariel is asked to make good some of these fine promises, he rebels. "Is there more toyle?" he asks,

> Since thou dost give me pains,
> Let me remember thee what thou hast promis'd
> Which is not yet perform'd me.

Prospero.   How now? moodie?
    What is't thou canst demand?

Ariel. My Libertie.

---

2 R. A. Brower, *The Fields of Light* (Oxford, 1951), p. 110.

Some critics have been disturbed at the vehemence of Prospero's reaction; and it is true that phrases such as "Thou liest, malignant Thing"—"my slave, as thou reportst thy selfe"—and "Dull thing, I say so" sound more suited for Caliban than delicate Ariel. Yet it is not really surprising that Prospero should display what Wilson calls "ebullitions of imperious harshness" toward a slave who, after such an enthusiastic declaration of willingness to serve him, balks at the first mention of "more worke."

Prospero does more than chide; he threatens punishment. Sycorax punished Ariel with confinement in a cloven pine—"it was a torment To lay upon the damn'd" —but Prospero threatens to go one step farther: "I will rend an Oake And peg—thee in his knotty entrailes. . . ." Ariel begs for pardon and promises to be "correspondent to command." He is rewarded with a fresh promise of freedom—"after two daies I will discharge thee"—and sent about his master's business with renewed imperiousness:

> goe take this shape
> And hither come in 't: goe: hence
> With diligence.

"*Exit*," reads the stage direction.

From this point on Ariel is correspondent to command, and his first service is to bring Ferdinand into the presence of Miranda. It is the traditional role of the intelligent slave to further his master's marriage projects, and Ariel fully regains Prospero's favor and gets a renewed promise of the traditional reward. "Delicate Ariel, Ile set thee free for this." In fact, Ariel gains a remission of part of his stated time: "Ile free thee Within two dayes for this."

Throughout the rest of the play Ariel acts as Prospero's eyes and ears, but, as befits the clever slave, with a certain initiative too. He rescues Alonso and Gonzalo from the conspirators, and his words suggest that, though he has a general commission to protect Gonzalo at any rate, the methods have been left to him. "Prospero my Lord, shall know what I have done." His mischievous action against Caliban and the two Neapolitans is apparently his own idea, for Prospero later asks him where they are, and Ariel gives a full report of the chase he has led them. Yet the comic aspects of the relationship between master and slave are not neglected in the swift action of the play's central section. Ariel, ordered to produce spirits for the masque, replies:

> Before you can say come, and goe,
> And breathe twice: and cry so, so:
> Each one tripping on his Toe,
> Will be here with mop, and mowe.

This sounds remarkably like the half-ironical servile exaggeration of the Plautine slave promising miracles of speed. Charmides orders his slave to go from Athens to Piraeus—*I, i, ambula, actutum redi,* "Go on, go on, start walking, come back right away"—and gets the answer, *Illic sum atque hic sum,* "I'm there and back again." And that same Ariel who asks "Doe you love me Master? no?" at the end of the jingle quoted above, can also admit that he fears his master's temper.

Prospero. Spirit: We must prepare to meet with Caliban.

Ariel. I my Commander, when I presented *Ceres*
I thought to have told thee of it, but I fear'd
Least I might anger thee.

The comic aspects of Ariel's slavery are balanced by those of Prospero's mastery. This is not the only reference to Prospero's short temper. "Why speakes my father so ungently?"—"he's compos'd of harshnesse"—"your fathers in some passion"—"never till this day Saw I him touch'd with anger, so distemper'd"—these observations only confirm the impression made by Prospero's outbursts of fury against his slaves. There is more than a touch in him of the Plautine old man, the irascible *senex* (*severus, difficilis, iratus, saevus,* as Donatus describes him),[3] who may in the end turn out to have a heart of gold, but who for the first four acts has only a noticeably short temper and a rough tongue.

This anger of Prospero is of course much more than a reminiscence of the irascibility of the stock comic figure: he is a man who has been grievously wronged, and who now, with his enemies at his mercy, intends to revenge himself. That this has been his intention is made perfectly clear in the speech in which that intention is forever renounced:

> Thogh with their high wrongs I am strook to th' quick
> Yet, with my nobler reason, gainst my furie
> Doe I take part: the rarer Action is
> In vertue, then in vengeance.

And this renunciation takes place when the slave rises superior to his master, setting an example of noble compassion:

Ariel. . . . your charm so strongly works 'em
  That if you now beheld them, your affections
  Would become tender.

Prospero. Dost thou thinke so, Spirit?

Ariel. Mine would, Sir, were I humane.

Prospero. And mine shall.

This is a magnificently imaginative version of the scenes in which the comedy slave surpasses the master in qualities which are traditionally those of the free man—in intelligence, courage, self-sacrifice. Here the nonhuman slave surpasses his human master in humanity.

As the play draws to a close, the recognition of Ariel's services and the renewed promises of liberation increase in frequency to become an obsessive burden:

---

[3] Cf. George F. Duckworth, *The Nature of Roman Comedy* (Princeton, 1952), p. 242, n. 14.

                                      thou
Shalt have the ayre at freedome: for a little
Follow, and doe me service.
                          quickly Spirit,
Thou shalt ere long be free.
                       I shall misse
Thee, but yet thou shalt have freedome.
Bravely (my diligence) thou shalt be free.

"The reluctance of the sylph to be under the command
even of Prospero," says Coleridge, "is kept up through
the whole play, and in the exercise of his admirable
judgment Shakespeare has availed himself of it in order
to give Ariel an interest in the event, looking forward
to that moment when he was to gain his last and only
reward—simple and eternal liberty." He might have
added that what Shakespeare "has availed himself of" is
a dramatic design as old as European comedy.

Ariel, the slave whose nature is free, is balanced by
Ferdinand, the free man and prince, who is enslaved.
Accused as "spy" and "traitor," he is subdued by Prospero's magic: but there is nothing magical about the
entertainment he is promised.

Ile manacle thy necke and feete together:
Sea water shalt thou drinke: thy food shall be
The fresh-brooke Mussels, wither'd roots, and huskes
Wherein the Acorne cradled. Follow.

This is a Shakespearean version of the chains and prison
diet with which the ancient comic slave is so often threatened, and of which he so often complains. And Ferdinand's next appearance shows him performing servile
tasks:

                         I must remove
Some thousands of these Logs, and pile them up,
Upon a sore injunction.

The work he is doing is in fact Caliban's work (*"Enter*

Caliban with a burthen of wood" is the stage direction
for the preceding scene), and Ferdinand himself describes it as "wodden slaverie." But whereas Caliban has
just declared his independence, and Ariel longs to be
free, Ferdinand the free man is for the moment content
to be a slave:

> all corners else o' th' Earth
> Let liberty make use of: space enough
> Have I in such a prison.

The service which he so willingly accepts is of course
not that of his master, but that of his mistress:

> The verie instant that I saw you, did
> My heart flie to your service, there resides
> To make me slave to it, and for your sake
> Am I this patient Logge-man.

And the multiple wit of these variations on the theme
is dazzlingly displayed when he and Miranda plight their
troth:

Miranda.   to be your fellow
  You may denie me, but Ile be your servant
  Whether you will or no.

Ferdinand. My Mistris (deerest)
  And I thus humble ever.

Miranda. My husband then?

Ferdinand. I, with a heart as willing
  As bondage ere of freedome: heere's my hand.

He accepts marriage (that is, bondage) with a heart "as
willing as bondage ere of freedome" (as willingly as
Ariel, for example, would accept his liberty), but this
acceptance, overheard by Prospero, is the signal for his
release from the "wodden slaverie" in which he is now
bound.

Ferdinand, as we have seen, is contrasted to Ariel, but Ariel's real opposite is Caliban, "my slave, who never yeelds us kinde answere." Caliban's employment is menial: while Ariel treads "the Ooze of the salt deepe," Caliban "do's make our fire Fetch in our wood, and serves in Offices That profit us." It is remarkable that in an island where spirits can be made to produce banquets and perform masks, Prospero should need the services of Caliban to "fetch in firing . . . scrape trenchering" and "wash dish," but so it is. "We cannot misse him."

Caliban, besides being a "Tortoys," "Hag-seed," a "delicate Monster," a "Moone-calfe," a "debosh'd Fish," and a "borne Devill," is also a slave, a poisonous, lying, and abhorred slave, to quote Prospero. His first speech offstage)—"There's wood enough within"—and the onstage curses which follow it are enough to suggest a familiar frame of reference for the first appearance of this outlandish figure: he is the surly, cursing slave of the old tradition.

Caliban's curses are highly original in expression—"language as hobgoblin as his person," says Dryden justly. Shakespeare has created a special vocabulary of invective appropriate to the savage apprehension of nature, but the expressions have the same dramatic characteristics as their venerable ancestors. The cursing seems to be a thing in and for itself—it violates plausibility, for one thing. Why should Prospero put up with it, and counter it with threats of punishment that sound curiously like it? And Caliban is made to refer to another aspect of this improbability; "his Spirits heare me, And yet I needes must curse." He "needes must curse" because his cursing is vital to the comic essence of his nature; the scene in which he exchanges curses for Prospero's threats of punishment is a traditional feature of the comedy of master and slave.

Caliban is a sullen slave (a Sceparnio), a cursing slave (a Toxilus), and he is also a lecherous one. The only touch of low sexual humor in *The Tempest* is Caliban's unrepentant laughter when reminded of his attempt on

Miranda's virtue: but that one laugh is enough to remind us that he has an ancestry reaching back through scurrilous Plautine slaves and Aristophanic comic actors wearing a leather *phallos* to the ithyphallic satyrs of the Greek vase paintings.

Caliban's meeting with Trinculo and Stephano is a servile parallel and parody of Miranda's meeting with Ferdinand; both mistress and slave are overcome with wonder at the vision of their counterparts in Neapolitan society. Miranda's worshiping remark, "I might call him A thing divine," is echoed in Caliban's "that's a brave God, and beares Celestiall liquor"; while Ferdinand's "My Language? Heavens" finds a base echo in Stephano's "where the divell should he learne our language?" Stephano and Trinculo—"two *Neapolitanes* scap'd"—are to Ferdinand as Caliban is to Miranda; creatures of lower order. And Stephano the "drunken butler" is a familiar figure; the slave in charge of his master's wine who drinks most of it himself is a standard character of the old comedy. In one of the better-known Plautine plays, the *Miles Gloriosus,* there is a scene with not one but two drunken butlers, one dead drunk on his back inside the house, the other drunk on his feet outside.

But the drunkenness of Stephano is surpassed by that of Caliban. His extravagant admiration of Stephano, as Trinculo perceives, is more than savage simplicity: "The poore Monster's in drinke." In his drunken fit he thinks of the primary objective of all slaves, his freedom. Unlike Ariel, he cannot hope to win it by delicate service, he can gain his freedom only by working against his master or by running away from him. He deserts Prospero, "the Tyrant that I serve," for Stephano, and the service of this new master turns out to be perfect freedom, which he proceeds to celebrate in song and dance. "Freedome, high-day, high-day, freedome." It is the traditional servile drunken exhibition and it is grotesquely funny, but it is only the other side of the coin which shows us Ariel, moody, demanding his liberty. Ariel and Caliban are opposite as earth and air, but they are both

nslaved, and in this they are alike. One suspects that
Caliban speaks something close to the truth when he tells
Stephano that Prospero's power depends on one thing
only, his "Bookes":

> without them
> Hee's but a Sot, as I am; nor hath not
> One Spirit to command: they all do hate him
> As rootedly as I.

"They say there's but five upon this Isle," says Trinculo. "We are three of them, if th' other two be brain'd
like us, the State totters." Of the three of them, the one
with the most brains is Caliban. With servile flattery and
cunning he supplants Trinculo in Stephano's graces, securing a series of reprimands and eventually a beating
for his fellow slave.

> Beate him enough: after a little time
> Ile beate him too.

He is now Stephano's "lieutenant," but he knows what
must be done to guarantee his new-found dignity: he
must encompass Prospero's death. And so the "foule
Conspiracy" is formed. The slaves indulge their exagger-
ated fantasies of freedom and sovereignty: "Monster, I
will kill this man: his daughter and I will be King and
Queene, save our Graces: and *Trinculo* and Thy selfe
shall be Vice-royes." It is a servile parody of the more
serious conspiracy of the free men, Antonio and Sebastian.

The drunken butler dreams of a kingdom; he is not
the first. It is instructive to compare his plans with those
of Gripus, the Plautine slave who has fished a treasure
out of the sea and intends to hang on to it:

> When I'm once free, I'll equip myself with property, an
> estate, a house. I'll go into trade with great ships; I'll be
> considered a King among Kings. . . . I'll build a great city,
> and call it Gripus, after myself, a monument to my fame

and doings. And in it I'll set up a great Kingdom . . . An
yet, King though I am, I must make my breakfast on sou
wine and salt, no relish for my bread.

This comic incongruity between the present and the imag
ined future, between station and ambition, is carried t
hilarious lengths in the climactic appearance of Caliba
and his associates. They "do smell all horse-pisse," bu
Stephano's royal dignity is undisturbed. "Wit shall no
goe unrewarded while I am King of this Country," he
says, and Trinculo hails him in the titles of the old ballad
"O King *Stephano,* O Peere: O worthy *Stephano.*" Stand
ing at the entrance to Prospero's cell King Stephano
talks like a tragic hero: "I do begin to have blood
thoughts." And Caliban's urgent warnings are rejected in
royal style: "Monster, lay to your fingers . . . or Ile turn
you out of my Kingdome."

A few seconds later Stephano's kingdom melts into
thin air. And on his last appearance he and Trinculo are
ordered off with Caliban to perform menial tasks; no
distinction is made between them.

> Goe Sirha, to my Cell,
> Take with you your Companions: as you looke
> To have my pardon, trim it handsomely.

The stupid slaves, their wild ambitions foiled and their
presumption suitably punished, are restored to their
proper place and function.

Prospero has already been recognized as "sometime
Millaine" and restored to his proper station—"thy dukedom I resigne"—the marriage of Ferdinand and Miranda
is arranged; all that remains is to free the clever slave—
"to the elements Be free, and fare thou well"—and the
play, except for a version of the conventional Plautine
request for applause, is over, the traditional paradigm
complete. Gonzalo is given the speech in which the loose
ends are tied together and the pattern of restoration
spelled out:

> In one voyage
> Did *Claribell* her husband finde at *Tunis*,
> And *Ferdinand* her brother, found a wife,
> Where he himselfe was lost: *Prospero* his Dukedome
> In a poore Isle:

So far we are still within the recognizable limits of the ancient plan, but Gonzalo's closing words (though they continue the metaphor of liberation) can serve to remind us that this plan is only the bare outline of a poetic structure which in feeling and imagination as far surpasses Plautine comedy as "great'st do's least":

> —*Prospero* his Dukedome
> In a poore Isle: and all of us, our selves,
> When no man was his owne.

REUBEN A. BROWER

The Mirror of Analogy: "The Tempest"

> The Mind, that Ocean where each kind
> Does streight its own resemblance find;
> Yet it creates, transcending these,
> Far other Worlds, and other Seas . . .
>
> ANDREW MARVELL

Of *The Tempest*, we may say what Ferdinand said of the masque,

> This is a most majestic vision, and
> Harmonious charmingly.

The harmony of the play lies in its metaphorical design, in the closeness and completeness with which its rich and varied elements are linked through almost inexhaustible analogies. It is hard to pick a speech at random without coming on an expression that brings us by analogy into direct contact with elements that seem remote because of their place in the action or because of the type of experience they symbolize. Opening the play at the second act we read,

From *Fields of Light* by Reuben A. Brower. New York: Oxford University Press, 1951. Copyright 1951 by Oxford University Press, Inc. Reprinted by permission.

Four legs and two voices; a most delicate monster!

The last phrase is comic enough as used of Caliban and as issuing from the lips of Stephano, a "most foul" speaker. But "delicate" evokes a more subtle incongruity by recalling characters and a world we might suppose were forgotten. Stephano is parodying Prospero when he rebukes Ariel as "a spirit too delicate / To act her [Sycorax's] earthy and abhorr'd commands" and when he says,

> delicate Ariel,
> I'll set thee free for this!

We have in Stephano's words not only the familiar Shakespearean balancing of comic and serious, but a counterpointing of analogies that run throughout the play. "Delicate" as the antithesis of "earth" points to the opposition of Ariel and Caliban and to the often recurring earth-air symbolism of *The Tempest*. "Delicate" used of this remarkable island creature echoes also the "delicate temperance" of which the courtiers spoke and "the air" that "breathes . . . here most sweetly." "Monster"—almost another name for Caliban—balances these airy suggestions with an allusion to "the people of the island . . . of monstrous shape" and thereby to the strain of fantastic sea lore in *The Tempest,* which is being parodied in this scene.

So viewed, Shakespeare's analogies may perhaps seem too much like exploding nebulae in an expanding though hardly ordered universe. But Shakespeare does not "multiply variety in a wilderness of mirrors"; he makes use of a few fairly constant analogies that can be traced through expressions sometimes the same and sometimes extraordinarily varied. And the recurrent analogies (or continuities) are linked through a key metaphor into a single metaphorical design. Shakespeare is continually prodding us—often in ways of which we are barely conscious— to relate the passing dialogue with other dialogues into and through a super-design of metaphor.

In concentrating on how the design is built up, I am

not forgetting that it is a metaphorical design in a *drama* that we are interested in how Shakespeare has linked stages in a presentation of changing human relationships Toward the end of the chapter I hope to show how wonderfully the metaphorical design is related to the main dramatic sequence of *The Tempest,* especially in the climactic speeches of Acts IV and V.

The play moves forward, we should remember, from a scene of tempest to a final promise of "calm seas, auspicious gales," and through a series of punishments or trials to a series of reconciliations and restorations. Although, as Dr. Johnson might say, there is a "concatenation of events" running through Prospero's "project" and though the play has a curiously exact time schedule, there is often little chronological or logical connection between successive dialogues or bits of action. To be sure Shakespeare has the Elizabethan conventions on his side, but the freedom of his dramatic composition in *The Tempest* never seems merely conventional or capricious because the linkage of analogy is so varied and so pervasive.

The surest proof of the pervasiveness of Shakespeare's design lies in the mere number of continuities that can be discovered in the play. But some are more important than others because they can be traced through more expressions or in more scenes and because they express analogies more closely related to the key metaphor. The six main continuities, roughly labeled to indicate their character, are: "strange-wondrous," "sleep-and-dream," "sea-tempest," "music-and-noise," "earth-air," "slavery-freedom," and "sovereignty-conspiracy."

All of these continuities appear during the second scene of Act I, which is an exposition of Shakespeare's metaphorical and dramatic designs for the entire play. Near the close of the scene, Ariel's two songs offer wonderfully concentrated expressions of both designs. "Come unto these yellow sands" calms the "fury" of the waves and Ferdinand's "passion," thus charting in brief the course of the action. "Full fathom five" is anticipatory in a very different fashion. It presents in miniature the main lines of the metaphorical design and sounds the key note of "sea change," Shakespeare's most direct expression of the key metaphor of *The Tempest*. [See I.ii.1–186.]

As we trace the first two continuities ("strange-wondrous," "sleep-and-dream"), the reader can appreciate how unobtrusively they emerge from the developing dramatic pattern. Prospero's narrative, with which the scene opens, tells us of the past and describes the present situation while symbolizing the quality of *The Tempest* world. Prospero explains that his enemies have come to this shore "by accident most strange," and Miranda, who falls to sleep at the end of his tale, accounts for her lapse by saying,

> The strangeness of your story put
> Heaviness in me.

Prospero's tale was strange indeed: it included a ruler "rapt in secret studies," a "false uncle" who "new created / The creatures" of the state, the miraculous voyage of Prospero and Miranda (who was "a cherubin") and their safe arrival "by Providence divine." This "strangeness" is best defined by Alonso's remarks near the end of the play:

> These are not natural events; they strengthen
> From strange to stranger...
>
> This is as strange a maze as e'er men trod;
> And there is in this business more than nature
> Was ever conduct of . . .

They are "unnatural" in a broad seventeenth-century sense of the term; that is, outside the order which includes all created things. The theme is almost constantly being played on: "strange," "strangely," or "strangeness" occur altogether some seventeen times, and similar meanings are echoed in "wondrous," "monstrous," "divine."

Of all the analogies of the play this is probably the vaguest, the nearest in effect to the atmospheric unity of nineteenth-century Romantic poetry. But a more precise metaphor of strangeness appears, the "strangeness" of "new created creatures." From the "accident most strange" of the shipwreck we come to Alonso's ponderous woe:

> O thou, mine heir
> Of Naples and of Milan! what strange fish
> Hath made his meal on thee?

and then to Trinculo's discovery of Caliban—"A strange fish!" With a similar comic antiphony, Miranda finds Ferdinand "a thing divine," and Ferdinand replies, "O you wonder"; while a little later Caliban hails Trinculo as his god and cries, "Thou wondrous man." The full significance of these strange births will appear later.

The vague "strangeness" of the island world is closely allied to a state of sleep, both continuities appearing in Miranda's remark about the "heaviness" that came over her while listening to Prospero's story. The feeling that we are entering on an experience of sleep-and-dream arises beautifully out of the dramatic and rhythmic texture of the opening dialogue between father and daughter. The movement of these speeches with their oddly rocking repetitions is in key with the sleepy incredibility of the events about to be described: "Canst thou remember... thou canst ... I can ... thy remembrance ... my remembrance ... thou remember'st ... Twelve year since, Miranda, twelve year since ..." Throughout the story Prospero is continually reminding Miranda to "attend" to the telling, and it seems perfectly natural that at the end she should be "inclin'd to sleep." (Note in passing how neatly Shakespeare has broken a long narrative into dialogue and also given a distinct impression of Prospero's firmness and of Miranda's innocent dependence.) Miranda's images of the past come back to her "rather like a dream," and Prospero seems to be drawing their story from a world of sleep, "the dark backward and abysm of time."

With the next scene (the mourning King and his courtiers) we meet one of Shakespeare's typical analogical progressions. The sleep which affects the courtiers is, like Miranda's, a strange "heaviness." Their dialogue runs down, psychologically and rhythmically, through three echoes of Miranda's words:

Gonzalo. Will you laugh me asleep, for I am very heavy?...

Sebastian. Do not omit the heavy offer of it . . .

Alonso. Thank you. Wondrous heavy.

Sebastian. What a strange drowsiness possesses them!

The conversation that follows between the conspirators shows how Shakespeare uses an analogy to move to a new level of action and experience and to make them harmonious with what precedes and follows. Sebastian and Antonio begin by talking about actual sleep and waking: why are they not drowsy like the others? Then Antonio shifts to talking of sleepiness and alertness of mind, and from that to imagining that he sees "a crown dropping" upon Sebastian's head. The wit becomes more complex as Sebastian describes Antonio's talk as "sleepy language"—without meaning—though indicating that it does have meaning, "There's meaning in thy snores." This dialogue, which readers are liable to dismiss as so much Elizabethan wit, has its place within the play's metaphorical pattern. The plotting takes on a preposterous dreamy-sleepy character like that of Prospero's narrative and Miranda's recollections. Through such verbal trifling Shakespeare maintains the continuous quality of his imagined world.

References to similar wakings and sleepings, to dreams and dreamlike states, abound from here to the end of the play, where the sailors are "brought moping . . . even in a dream," and the grand awakening of all the characters is completed. But up to that point confusion between waking and sleep is the rule, being awake is never far from sleep or dream. In *The Tempest* sleep is always imminent, and more than once action ends in sleep or trance.

The witty talk of the conspirators glides from conceits of "sleep" to conceits of "the sea," to talk of "standing water" and "flowing" and "ebbing." The "good Gonzalo," in consoling the King, speaks in similar figures:

> It is foul weather in us all, good sir,
> When you are cloudy.

Recurrent expressions of "sea and tempest," like those of "sleep and dream," are numerous and have a similar atmospheric value of not letting us forget the special quality of life on Prospero's island. But they also have far more important effects, for many of them become metaphors which are more precisely and more variously symbolic and which link more kinds of experience together.

By tracing two groups of "tempest" expressions, metaphors of "sea-swallowing" and images of "clouds," we may understand how these more complex analogies are built up. We may also see how Shakespeare moves from narrative fact to metaphor, from image or metaphor referring only to narrative fact to metaphor rich in moral and psychological implications. As in creating the analogies of "strangeness" and "sleep," Shakespeare starts from a dramatic necessity: the audience must be told what the situation was in the storm scene with which the play opens, and they must learn through an actor (Miranda) how they are to take it. (See I.ii.1–186.) Although there is a hint of magic in Miranda's vision of the tempest, she pictures it as a violent actuality:

> Had I been any god of power, I would
> Have sunk the sea within the earth, or e'er
> It should the good ship so have swallow'd and
> The fraughting souls within her.

As if there were an inner rhythm in these responses, this metaphor, like others we have been tracing, recurs in the plotting episode. Antonio is speaking of his sister Claribel, left behind in Tunis:

>   she that from whom
> We all were sea-swallow'd, though some cast again,
> And by that destiny to perform an act
> Whereof what's past is prologue, what to come
> In yours and my discharge.

In this new context "sea-swallowed" does several things at once. It brings back Miranda's horrified impression; but the magical nature of the storm now being known, the phrase reminds us that there was no "sea-swallowing," no actual sinking of "fraughting souls." Next, with a curiously Shakespearean "glide and a jump" via the pun on "cast," "sea-swallowed" merges into another metaphor (they are now "cast" as actors in destiny's drama). "Sea-swallowing" has become a metaphor that expresses destiny's extraordinary way of bringing Sebastian to the throne.

The irony of Antonio's words, which is clear to the audience, is made explicit later in the solemn speech in which Ariel explains the purpose of the tempest:

> You are three men of sin, whom Destiny—
> That hath to instrument this lower world
> And what is in 't—the never-surfeited sea
> Hath caused to belch up you . . .

Few passages could show better how Shakespeare carries his analogies along and at the same time completely renews them. The "belching up" recalls the wreck and the casting ashore and the earlier connection with destiny. But the sea's action is now described in much grosser terms and with grim sarcasm, while the oddly compact grammar makes "the never-surfeited sea" very nearly a synonym for "Destiny." The violence though increased is now religious and moral; the imagery has become expressive of the strenuous punishment and purification of "three men of sin."[1] So by the continuity of his varying metaphor Shakespeare has expressed an unbroken transition from actual storm to the storm of the soul. This sequence, which expresses both physical and metaphysical transformations, points very clearly to the key metaphor of *The Tempest.*

The recurrent cloud images present a similar sequence as they take on various symbolic meanings in the course of the play. "Cloud" does not actually occur in the open-

[1] Alonso, Antonio, Sebastian.

ing storm scene, but when Trinculo sees "another storm
brewing" and speaks of a "black cloud," we are reminded
of the original tempest. The cloud undergoes an appropriate change in Trinculo's speech; it "looks like a foul
bombard that would shed his liquor." This comic cloud is
very different from "the curl'd clouds" on which Ariel
rides, though they too are associated with storms. The
clouds of Caliban's exquisite speech are those of Ariel
and the deities of the masque:

> and then, in dreaming,
> The clouds methought would open and show riches
> Ready to drop upon me . . .

Clouds—here linked with magical riches—become in
Prospero's "cloud-capp'd towers" speech a symbol for
the unsubstantial splendor of the world. One of the sub-
ordinate metaphors there, the "melting into air" and the
"dissolving" of the clouds, is picked up in Prospero's
later words about the courtiers:

> The charm dissolves apace;
> And as the morning steals upon the night,
> Melting the darkness, so their rising senses
> Begin to chase the ignorant fumes that mantle
> Their clearer reason.

This dissolution of night clouds (suggested also by
"fumes") is a figure for the change from madness to
sanity, from evil ignorance to the clear perceptions of
reason. Although the cloud images of the play are so
varied, they have a common symbolic value, for whether
they are clouds of tempest or of visionary riches or of the
soul, they are always magically unsubstantial. The reader
is led to feel some touch of likeness among experiences
as different as a storm at sea, a bit of drunken whimsy,
a vision of heavenly and earthly beauty, and a spiritual
regeneration. The cloud sequence, as an arc of metaphor,
is in perfect relation to the gradual dramatic movement
from tempest and punishment to fair weather and recon-

ciliation, the images having meanings more and more remote from any actual storm.

The "cloudlike" change in the distracted souls of the guilty nobles was induced (as if in reminiscence of Plato) by *Solemn music*—

> A solemn air and the best comforter
> To an unsettled fancy.

Many of the expressions referring to music, like the stage direction above, are not explicitly metaphorical, but along with the continuities of "sleep" and "strangeness" they help maintain the magical character of the action. The music is always the music of spirits and always a sign of more than natural events.

The one fairly constant musical metaphor[2] in *The Tempest* is the symbolic opposition of confused noises, especially storm sounds, and harmonious music. The key word and the central impression of the opening scene is certainly "noise"[3] in the modern sense. The impression is carried over in the first words of the next scene:

> If by your art, my dearest father, you have
> Put the wild waters in this roar, allay them.

Miranda's request is soon answered by Ariel's first song, "the wild waves" are "whist." The *solemn and strange music* heard when the *strange Shapes* bring a banquet to the courtiers makes Alonso say, "What harmony is this? my good friends, hark!" Gonzalo replies: "Marvelous sweet music!" By contrast, when Ariel enters shortly

---

2 The music and tempest metaphors have been traced in a very different fashion and with quite different aims by G. Wilson Knight in *The Shakespearian Tempest*. My analysis (which I had worked out before reading Professor Knight's essay) has a more limited purpose: to show a continuity of analogy and a development of metaphor parallel to that of the other continuities I have traced.

3 The scene is full of expressions such as: *A tempestuous noise of thunder and lightning heard,* "roarers," "command these elements to silence," *A cry within,* "A plague upon this howling! they are louder than the weather, or our office," "insolent noisemaker," *A confused noise within,* et cetera.

after, in order to inform the "three men of sin" of thei
punishment by the storm, there is an offstage sound o
Thunder and lightning. The masque vision which Ferdi
nand finds "harmonious charmingly" is rudely interrupted
by *a strange, hollow, and confused noise* which symbolize
the stormy anger expressed by Prospero in the speeche
that follow. When in the next scene he prepares to forgive
his enemies, he abjures the "rough magic" by which he

> call'd forth the mutinous winds,
> And 'twixt the green sea and the azur'd vault
> Set roaring war . . .

As the *solemn music* is played the clouds of ignorance
"dissolve," and so the musical metaphor, like the sea
metaphor, has moved from outer to inner weather.

The music analogy has some close links with the earth-
air continuity which we glanced at in the introductory
chapter of the book. Ferdinand, following Ariel's "yellow
sands" song, asks, "Where should this music be? i' th
air, or th' earth?" And a little later:

> This is no mortal business, nor no sound
> That the earth owes: I hear it now above me.

The connection of air and music can never be long forgotten: Ariel and his spirits of "thin air" are the musi-
cians of the island.

The earth-air, Caliban-Ariel antithesis coincides at
points with what we might call a slavery-freedom continuity, for Caliban is in Prospero's words both "slave"
and "earth." Ariel too is called a "slave"[4] by Prospero
and for the time of the play he is as much a slave a
Caliban. He is always asking for his freedom, which i
at last granted, his release being symbolically expressed
in the airy rovings of his final song. He flies into perpetua
summer and, like air, becomes merged with the elements

---

4 Both are called "slaves" in Act I. ii, the scene of metaphorical expo
sition.

By contrast, the "high-day, freedom!" of which Caliban sings is ironically enough simply a change of masters.

The "slaves" and "servants" of the play suffer various kinds of imprisonment, from Ariel in his "cloven pine" to Ferdinand's mild confinement, and before the end of Act IV everyone except Prospero and Miranda has been imprisoned in one way or another. During the course of Act V all the prisoners except Ferdinand (who has already been released) are set free, each of them by Prospero's special command.

A sovereignty-conspiracy analogy parallels very closely the slavery-freedom analogy, some of the same persons, e.g., Ferdinand and Caliban, appearing as both slaves and conspirators. "That foul conspiracy/ Of the beast Caliban, and his confederates" is of course a parody version of the "Open-ey'd Conspiracy" of Sebastian and Antonio. Ferdinand, too, is charged fantastically by Prospero with plotting against his island rule. Talk of kings and royalty turns up in many scenes, being connected usually with the denial of kingship, as in "good Gonzalo's" speech on his golden-age commonwealth where "he would be king" and yet have "no sovereignty." Though no single explicit metaphor for conspiracy or usurpation is often repeated, Shakespeare rings many changes on the theme as he moves from plot to plot. Prospero's brother, we recall, is said to have "new created the creatures" of state. Alonso's seizure of power is called a "substitution": "crediting his own lies," he began to believe "he was indeed the duke," and from merely playing a part he went on to become "absolute Milan." The figure is picked up in the somnolent dialogue of Sebastian and Antonio:

> I remember
> You did supplant your brother Prospero.

In the second of the scenes in which Caliban and his fellows plot to overthrow the island "tyrant," Sebastian's "supplant" is recalled with a difference:

Caliban. I would my valiant master would destroy thee; I do not lie.

Stephano. Trinculo, if you trouble him any more in his tale, by this hand, I will supplant some of your teeth.

The figure recurs a little later in a more serious context:

>   . . . you three
> From Milan did supplant good Prospero.

In Act V after various supplantings, serious and comic, accomplished or merely projected, all true kings are restored and all false ones dethroned.

The two continuities, sovereignty-conspiracy and slavery-freedom, are also alike in the fact that their metaphorical force is expressed through scenes that are just one step removed from allegory. The more serious of the restorations and releases convey similar kinds of moral meaning. Ferdinand's release from "wooden slavery" signifies that he is a true lover and a true prince. In being freed from madness Alonso has escaped from "heartsorrow" and regained his rightful rank and a "clear life ensuing." Both continuities convey an impression of topsy-turvydom in the order of things, an unnatural interchange of status among creatures of every kind. Both express a return to stability after a disturbance of degree.

What then is the key metaphor through which the various continuities are linked, and how are they connected through it? Shakespeare's most direct expression of his key metaphor is "sea change," the key phrase of Ariel's song. But what does Shakespeare mean by "sea change"? Ariel sings of "bones" being made into "coral" and of "eyes" becoming "pearls." "A change into something rich and strange," we now understand, is a change "out of nature." "Sea change" is a metaphor for "magical transformation," for metamorphosis. The key metaphor of the play is "change" in this special sense, and "change" is the analogy common to all of the continuities we have been tracing. (I am not forgetting that they are also expressive of many other relationships, or that Shakespeare

is often playing with two or three metaphors at once, as
in the various figures of "sea-swallowing." But all are at
least expressive of change, or changeableness.)

Through the first rather vague analogies we traced, of
"strangeness" and "sleep-and-dream," numerous events
and persons in the play are qualified as belonging to a
realm where anything may happen. Expressions of
"strangeness" and "sleep," like many of the references
to sea and music, suggest "far other Worlds and other
Seas," where magical change is to be expected. A more
particular metaphor of change is expressed through the
stress on the "strangeness" of "new creations" and on
the confusion between sleep and dream and waking. The
island is a world of fluid, merging states of being and
forms of life. This lack of dependable boundaries between
states is also expressed by the many instances of confusion between natural and divine. Miranda says that she
might call Ferdinand

> A thing divine; for nothing natural
> I ever saw so noble.

Ferdinand cannot be sure whether she is a goddess or a
maid, and Caliban takes Trinculo for a "brave god."
There is a further comic variation on this theme in Trinculo's difficulty in deciding whether to classify Caliban as
fish or man, monster or devil.

But "change" is most clearly and richly expressed
through the sequence of tempest images (especially
"cloud" and "sea-swallowed") and through the noise-
music antithesis. All kinds of sounds, harmonious and
ugly, like the manifestations of sea and storm, are expressive of magical transformation. "The fire and cracks/
Of sulfurous roaring" (imagery in which both storm and
sound analogies are blended) "infects" the courtiers'
"reason," and *solemn music* induces the "clearing" of
their understanding. The "music" and the "tempest" continuities, taken together as metaphors of "sea change,"
are perhaps the most extensive of all the analogies in their
organizing power. They recur often, they connect a wide

diversity of experiences, and they express in symbolic form some of the main steps in the drama, in particular, the climactic moments of inner change: Ariel's revelation to the courtiers of their guilt, Alonso's first show of remorse, and the final purification.

The earth-air or Caliban-Ariel antithesis may seem to have very little to do with metamorphosis. But the relation of this theme to the key metaphor is clear and important. Air, Ariel, and his music are a blended symbol of change as against the unchanging Caliban, "the thing of darkness." He can be punished, but hardly humanized; he is, says Prospero,

> A devil, a born devil, on whose nature
> Nurture can never stick; on whom my pains,
> Humanely taken, are all lost, quite lost.

The other continuities parallel to earth-air, of slavery-freedom and conspiracy-sovereignty, are frequently expressive of major and minor changes of status among the inhabitants and temporary visitors on Prospero's island.

But the interconnection of Shakespeare's analogies through the key metaphor cannot be adequately described, since we are able to speak of only one point of relationship at a time. We can get a better sense of the felt union of various lines of analogy in *The Tempest* by looking at the two passages where Shakespeare expresses his key metaphor most completely, the "Full fathom five" song and Prospero's "cloud-capp'd towers" speech.

Rereading Ariel's song at this point, we can see how many of the main continuities are alluded to and related in the description of "sea change" and how the song anticipates the metaphorical design that emerges through the dialogue of the whole play. The total metaphorical pattern is to an amazing degree an efflorescence from this single crystal:

> Full fathom five thy father lies;
> Of his bones are coral made:

Those are pearls that were his eyes:
Nothing of him that doth fade,
But doth suffer a sea change
Into something rich and strange.
Sea nymphs hourly ring his knell:
            Burthen: "Ding-dong!"
Hark! now I hear them—Ding-dong, bell.

In addition to the more obvious references to the deep
sea and its powers and to the "strangeness" of this drowning, there are indirect anticipations of other analogies.
"Fade" prefigures the "dissolving cloud" metaphor and
the theme of tempest changes, outer and inner. "Rich,"
along with "coral" and "pearls," anticipates the opulent
imagery of the dream-world passages and scenes, the
"riches ready to drop" on Caliban and the expressions
of wealth[5] and plenty in the masque. The song closes
with the nymphs tolling the bell, the transformation and
the "sea sorrow" are expressed through sea music. Ferdinand's comment reminds us that the song has connec-
tions with two other lines of analogy:

The ditty does remember my drown'd father.
This is no mortal business, nor no sound
That the earth owes:—I hear it now above me.

The song convinces Ferdinand that he is now King of
Naples (the first of the interchanges of sovereignty), and
it is a "ditty" belonging not to the "earth," but to the
"air."

The sense of relationship between the many continuities is still more vividly felt in the lines of Prospero's
most memorable speech:

You do look, my son, in a mov'd sort,
As if you were dismay'd: be cheerful, sir:
Our revels now are ended. These our actors,
As I foretold you, were all spirits and
Are melted into air, into thin air:

[5] "Rich" and "riches" occur no less than five times in the masque.

> And, like the baseless fabric of this vision,
> The cloud-capp'd towers, the gorgeous palaces,
> The solemn temples, the great globe itself,
> Yea, all which it inherit, shall dissolve
> And, like this insubstantial pageant faded,
> Leave not a rack behind. We are such stuff
> As dreams are made on, and our little life
> Is rounded with a sleep.

In Prospero's words Shakespeare has gathered all the lights of analogy into a single metaphor which sums up the metaphorical design and the essential meaning of *The Tempest*. The language evokes nearly every continuity that we have traced. "Melted into air," "dissolve," "cloud," and "rack" bring us immediately to Ariel and tempest changes, while "vision," "dream," and "sleep" recall other familiar continuities. "Revels," "gorgeous palaces," and "pageant" (for Elizabethans closely associated with royalty) are echoes of the kingly theme; and "solemn" is associated particularly with the soft music of change. The "stuff" of dreams is at once cloud-stuff (air) and cloth, both images being finely compressed in "baseless fabric." Taken with "faded" these images refer obliquely to the garments so miraculously "new-dyed . . . with salt water," one of the first signs of "sea change" noted by Gonzalo. Within the metaphor of tempest-clearing and of cloudlike transformation, Shakespeare has included allusions to every important analogy of change in the play.

But it is through the twofold progress of the whole figure that the change metaphor is experienced and its most general meaning fully understood. We read first: that like the actors and scenery of the vision, earth's glories and man shall vanish into nothingness. Through a happy mistake we also read otherwise. By the time we have passed through "dissolve," "insubstantial," and "faded," and reached "leave not a rack behind," we are reading "cloudcapped towers" in reverse as a metaphor of towerlike clouds. "Towers," "palaces," "temples," "the great globe," "all which it inherit" are now taken for cloud forms.

Through a sort of Proustian[6] merging of icon and subject, we experience the blending of states of being, of substantial and unsubstantial, or real and unreal, which is the essence of *The Tempest* metamorphosis.

Similar meanings are expressed through the closing dream figure, which grows equally out of the metaphorical context of the speech and the play. "Rounded," we should take with Kittredge as "surrounded," but without losing the force of round, as in Donne's "surrounded with tears." "Our little life" is more than sentimental, it is our little life (microcosm) in contrast with "the great globe" (macrocosm). There may also be an over-image in "surrounded" of the world in classical myth and geography with its encircling ocean, sleep being the stream that "rounds" the lesser world. In relation to the metaphorical design of the play, "rounded with a sleep" and the notion of life ending in dreams express again the sense of confusion between sleep and dream and waking. This metaphor which completes the figure of cloud-change is Shakespeare's most perfect symbol for the closeness of states that to our daylight sense are easily separable. Although the vision here expressed goes far beyond the play, it is still a natural extension of the dramatic moment and a fulfillment of the metaphor that has been implicit since the noisy opening lines of *The Tempest*.

But if Shakespeare's total metaphor is in a sense present everywhere, it is also a design that develops in close relation to the main dramatic movement of the play. As we have noted more than once, a particular metaphor will be varied to fit a new dramatic situation and so serve to express the situation more fully and to anticipate the next step in the development of the drama. The best example of this adaptation of metaphor comes in a speech in which Shakespeare seems to be playing capriciously with his noise-music theme. At first sight the passage seems inconsistent with the symbolic contrast between storm noise and music:

6 This merging in Proust was brought to my attention by J. I. Merrill in [an unpublished honors thesis done at Amherst].

Alonso.   O, it is monstrous! monstrous!
   Methought the billows spoke and told me of it;
   The winds did sing it to me; and the thunder,
   That deep and dreadful organ pipe, pronounc'd
   The name of Prosper: it did bass my trespass.

It is admittedly odd that the confused noise of the tempest should, in Alonso's soul, compose a harmony—however gloomy—but the paradox fits in perfectly with the developing structure of the play. Alonso has just been told by Ariel that the storm had a purpose as an instrument of Destiny. Since at this moment remorse first appears in the play and the inner clearing begins, it is exactly right that the storm sounds should seem harmonious and so point forward to the events of the fourth and fifth acts. No use of metaphor in *The Tempest* reveals more clearly Shakespeare's exact sense of the movement of his drama, of the changing human relations and feelings he is presenting.

In building up his metaphorical design, Shakespeare prepares us for the moment in *The Tempest* when the major shift in dramatic relationships takes place. The moment comes in the speech in which Prospero describes the behavior of the King and the courtiers as they slowly return from madness to sanity. The first important step toward this climax, Alonso's acknowledgment of his guilt, was expressed through a metaphor combining both sea and musical changes. The next step, Ferdinand's release from his tempest-trials and from dreamlike enchantment, is expressed through the masque, which is an elaborate dramatization of metamorphosis, Ariel's "meaner fellows," "the rabble," being now transformed into majestic Olympian goddesses. Once again, familiar continuities appear, and again they are transformed to fit a new occasion. "Earth," for example, is no longer "barren place and fertile," but the earth enriched by human cultivation and symbolized now by Ceres—not by Caliban, who is "nature resisting nurture." Iris summons this new Earth in the gorgeous speech beginning "Ceres, most bounteous lady, thy rich leas . . . ," lines in which we hear a quite new majesty of tone and movement. The couplet form sets the dialogue apart from human speech, while the longer periods, the added stresses, the phrasal balancings are especially appropriate to "that large utterance of the early gods." (Here is one of many instances of how Shakespeare adapts his sound patterns to his metaphorical and dramatic designs.) Prospero's visionary speech that ends "the revels" is not simply a concentration of metaphor without reference to the dramatic development. It announces the changes to come, it gives a rich expression of their meaning, and it anticipates the dreamlike flux of the psychological events of the last act.

If we now read Prospero's words in Act V, in which he describes the great changes as they take place, we see many references back to Shakespeare's metaphorical preparation for this moment. We also realize that various lines of action and various lines of analogy are converging almost simultaneously. The speech opens with Prospero's farewell to his art, after which he turns his thoughts to "restoring the senses" of the courtiers, whom Ariel has just gone to release:

A solemn air and the best comforter
To an unsettled fancy, cure thy brains,
Now useless, boil'd within thy skull! There stand,
For you are spell-stopp'd.
Holy Gonzalo, honorable man,
Mine eyes, even sociable to the show of thine,
Fall fellowly drops. The charm dissolves apace;
And as the morning steals upon the night,
Melting the darkness, so their rising senses
Begin to chase the ignorant fumes that mantle
Their clearer reason. O good Gonzalo!
My true preserver, and a loyal sir
To him thou follow'st, I will pay thy graces
Home, both in word and deed. Most cruelly
Didst thou, Alonso, use me and my daughter:
Thy brother was a furtherer in the act;
Thou'rt pinch'd for 't now, Sebastian. Flesh and blood,
You, brother mine, that entertain'd ambition,

Expell'd remorse and nature; who, with Sebastian—
Whose inward pinches therefore are most strong—
Would here have kill'd your king; I do forgive thee,
Unnatural though thou art! Their understanding
Begins to swell, and the approaching tide
Will shortly fill the reasonable shores
That now lie foul and muddy. Not one of them
That yet looks on me, or would know me. Ariel,
Fetch me the hat and rapier in my cell: [Exit Ariel.
I will discase me, and myself present,
As I was sometime Milan. Quickly, spirit;
Thou shalt ere long be free.

If this is a climactic moment, what changes in dramatic relationships are taking place, what is happening dramatically? The "men of sin," like Ferdinand, have come to the end of the trials which began with the storm and continued through various "distractions." Now, as Prospero explains, they are undergoing a moral as well as a mental regeneration, they are "pinch'd" with remorse and are being forgiven. The twofold regeneration is further dramatized in the speeches that follow: "th' affliction of Alonso's mind amends," he resigns Prospero's dukedom and "entreats" him to pardon his "wrongs."

But these are the prose facts, the bare bones of the changes in dramatic relationships. We cannot feel the peculiar quality of what is taking place or grasp its meaning apart from the metaphorical language through which it is being expressed. And the expressions acquire their force and precision from the whole metaphorical preparation we have been tracing. The courtiers' senses are restored by "an airy charm," by magic similar to that which was worked by Ariel and his spirits. The allusions to "heavenly music" and "a solemn air," in contrast to the "rough magic" that Prospero has abjured, remind us that these changes will be musically harmonious, like the songs of Ariel, and not noisy and confused like the storm sent to punish these men and reveal their "monstrous" guilt. Toward the end of the speech, the imagery recalls the tempest metaphor, but it is altered so as to

express the mental and moral change that is taking place.
The return of understanding is like an approaching tide
that covers the evidence of a storm (both "foul" and
"muddy" have storm associations from earlier occur-
rences).

But the metaphor that best expresses this clearing is
the one for which the preparation has been most complete:

> The charm dissolves apace;
> And as the morning steals upon the night,
> Melting the darkness, so their rising senses
> Begin to chase the ignorant fumes that mantle
> Their clearer reason.

"Dissolving" and "melting" and "fumes" take us back
at once to the grand transformations of the masque
speech, to the earlier cloud transformations both serious
and comic; and they take us back further to the association of clouds with magical tempests, inner storms,
and clearing weather. We read of the moral and psychological transformations with a present sense of these analogies. They are qualified for us as a dreamlike dissolution
of tempest clouds, as events in the "insubstantial" region
where reality and unreality merge.

It is through such links that Shakespeare concentrates
at this climactic moment the fullest meaning of his key
metaphor. There is of course no separation in the reader's
experience between the dramatic fact and the metaphorical qualification. The images that recur in Prospero's
speech take us back to felt qualities, but to felt qualities
embedded in particular dramatic contexts. "Melting," for
example, carries us to the spiritlike dissolution of "spirits
. . . melted into air, into thin air"; but it also reminds
us of the masque pageantry and of Prospero's calming
of Ferdinand's fears. We hear Prospero's soothing and
mysterious tone in both the earlier and later uses of the
word. The dramatic links and the analogical links are
experienced at once, which is to say that metaphorical
design and dramatic design are perfectly integrated.

We can now realize that metamorphosis is truly the key metaphor to the *drama,* and not the key metaphor to a detachable design of decorative analogies. Through the echoes in Prospero's speech of various lines of analogy, Shakespeare makes us feel each shift in dramatic relationships as a magical transformation, whether it is the courtiers' return to sanity, or Prospero's restoration to his dukedom, or Ariel's flight into perpetual summer. While all of the "slaves" and "prisoners" are being freed, and while all of the "sovereigns" are being restored, the sense of magical change is never wholly lost. The union of drama and metaphor in *The Tempest* is nowhere more complete than in the last act of the play.

The larger meaning of Shakespeare's total design, which was anticipated in the cloud and dream metaphor of Prospero's visionary speech, is most clearly and fully expressed in these final transformations. In a world where everything may become something else, doubts naturally arise, and in the swift flow of change the confusion about what is and what is not becomes fairly acute. When Prospero "discases" himself and appears as Duke of Milan, Gonzalo says with understandable caution:

> Whether this be,
> Or be not, I'll not swear.

And Prospero answers:

> You do yet taste
> Some subtilties o' the isle, that will not let you
> Believe things certain.

Whereas in the earlier acts the characters had often accepted the unreal as real (spirits, shipwrecks, drownings, visions), they now find it difficult to accept the real as truly real. The play concludes with their acceptance of the unexpected change to reality. But for the spectator there remains the heightened sense of the "thin partitions" that "do divide" these states. The world that common sense regards as real, of order in nature and society and of sanity in the individual, is a shimmering transformation of disorder. "We shall all be changed, in a moment, in the twinkling of an eye." (This or something like it is as near as we can come to describing the total attitude conveyed by *The Tempest*.)

Thus *The Tempest* is, like Marvell's "Garden," a Metaphysical poem of metamorphosis,[7] though the meaning of change is quite different for the two writers. It is worth noting too that Shakespeare "had Ovid in his eye," a fact that is obvious from the echoes of Golding's famous translation. There could be no better proof of Shakespeare's maturity than the contrast between the "sweet witty" Ovidianism of "Venus and Adonis" and the metaphorical design of *The Tempest,* which gives philosophic meaning to a drama of Ovidian metamorphosis. We remember "a lily prison'd in a jail of snow" as an isolated "beauty," but hardly as an apt symbol of the amorous relations of Venus and Adonis, or as symbolic of some larger meaning in their story. (Indeed a "jail of snow" is rather inept for the fervid goddess of the poem.) "Those were pearls that were his eyes" revives Ariel's sea music, Ferdinand's melancholy, and a world of fantasy and transshifting states of being. The increased concentration in meaning of the image from *The Tempest* is a sign of a growth in the command of language which is command of life for a poet. As Arnold said of Wordsworth, Shakespeare now "deals with more of *life*" and "he deals with *life,* as a whole, more powerfully." His maturity and power appear in the variety of experience so perfectly harmonized through the imaginative design of *The Tempest*.

7 See the excellent analysis of the poem in M. C. Bradbrook and M. G. Lloyd Thomas: *Andrew Marvell* (Cambridge, 1940), pp. 59–64.

DAVID WILLIAM

from *"The Tempest"* on the Stage

STAGING, COSTUME, AND MUSIC

On 5th November 1897, William Poel produced *The Tempest* for the Elizabethan Stage Society in the Mansion House. Shaw's review of the production may serve as an apt introduction to the problems of staging the play:

> Mr. Poel says frankly, "See that singers' gallery up there. Well, let's pretend that it's the ship." We agree, and the thing is done. But how could we agree to such a pretense with a stage ship? Before it we should say, "Take that thing away: if our imagination is to create a ship, it must not be contradicted by something that apes a ship so vilely as to fill us with denial and repudiation of the imposture. . . ." The reason is not that a man can *always* imagine things more vividly than art can present them to him, but that it takes an altogether extraordinary degree of art to compete with the pictures which the imagination makes when it is stimulated by such potent

From *Jacobean Theatre: Stratford-upon-Avon Studies I*, ed. John Russell Brown and Bernard Harris. London: Edward Arnold (Publishers) Ltd., 1960; New York: St Martin's Press, Inc., 1961. Reprinted by permission of Edward Arnold (Publishers) Ltd.

forces as the maternal instinct, superstitious awe, or the poetry of Shakespeare . . . . It requires the nicest judgment to know exactly how much help the imagination wants. There is no general rule, not even for any particular author. You can do best without scenery in *The Tempest* and *A Midsummer Night's Dream*, because the best scenery you can get will only destroy the illusion created by the poetry; but it does not at all follow that scenery will not improve a representation of *Othello*.

Poel's strict Elizabethanism is still unacceptable to most modern producers of Shakespeare. But recently there are signs that Shakespeare behind the proscenium arch is declining in favor. The splendid open stage at the Mermaid Theater has as yet only been used for a perversion of Shakespeare, but that and the modifications to the Stratford-upon-Avon stage are hopeful signs that the ascendancy of pictorial Shakespeare is at least being questioned. Certainly the basic facilities of the Elizabethan stage (provided, for example, in the stage at Stratford, Ontario) are appropriate to all the mechanical requirements of *The Tempest*. The inner stage for Prospero's cell, the various galleries for Ariel as harpy, the appearance of Juno, the hell trap for the ship's cabins (and Caliban's rock?), and the platform for the main action. No modern proscenium stage can match its opportunities for swift, continuous action and that flexibly intimate style of speech which so much of the text requires. The problem of speaking Prospero's text in I. ii is enormously increased by the distances between actor and audience in our proscenium theaters—and the apron stages at Stratford and the Old Vic are only slight modifications. The Elizabethan stage (or, to be more practical, a stage which preserves its advantages, adding to them needful modern facilities of sound and lighting) rightly throws all stress on the play itself. Anyone who has seen Shakespeare performed in these circumstances, or "in the round," is struck by the instant gain in intimacy and access to the play.

Given a proscenium stage, however, producers should

aim for a setting which accords as closely as possible with the play's structure. Presumably a basically permanent set will be an initial prerequisite, and no alterations to this during the play should be obtrusive or hold up the action. Designers should be restrained from trying to transgress the play's scenic data ("this bare island") and smothering the play with subaqueous gewgaws and the rest of the botanical farrago. But gorgeousness and mystery should accompany the Masque, and it is up to the collective ingenuities of producer, designer, and choreographer to ensure that the audience shall be no less transported than Ferdinand.

Distinctive costumes can do much to strengthen the play's impact. One should not dogmatize here beyond certain essentials which the text makes plain. The lords are the easiest problem. The prime requisite is clothes that will establish their social identities. Seventeenth-century contemporary style (English or European) would place the real world firmly (and becomingly) in the play's visual scheme. The islanders are less straightforward. We know that among his luggage Prospero was enabled to include:

> Rich garments, linens, stuffs, and necessaries,
> Which since have steaded much . . .
>
> (I.ii.164–65)

So, if these are to be seen, they must obviously harmonize in style with what the courtiers wear—though an inventive designer may find it helpful to point the passage of twelve years by changes in fashion for the latest visitors to the island.

For the denouement, Prospero must have a royal robe of Milan. If the transformation from the master of a full poor cell to Duke restored is to have the strongest impact possible, then there is a good argument in favor of Prospero's earlier costume being markedly different in style from the courtiers'. His condition of scholar and recluse may provide the designer with helpful points of

departure. And, of course, the magic garment must carry
the right associations of power and mystery. Miranda,
too, will benefit from whatever appearance of detachment
from the style of the "real" world can be designed that
is both apt and becoming.

A good many Ariels resort to varying degrees of un-
dress, offset by bizarre tones of body make-up and sundry
articles of vegetation. It is, however, salutary to remember that, nearly always, the more clothes are removed the
less spiritual the appearance becomes. Perhaps an apter
approach to the very difficult problem of designing for
Ariel may be to begin with the salient features of his
dramatic condition—"an airy spirit," once imprisoned in
a pine, aspiring towards total liberty, rapid transformation. The elemental associations are air and fire:

> I flamed amazement: sometime I'd divide
> And burn in many places . . .
> > (I.ii.198–99)

> Hast thou, which art but air . . .
> > (V.i.21)

The disguises of water nymph and harpy are explicit and
therefore easier to encompass.

Caliban's elements, on the other hand, are earth and
water, and the "salvage and deformed slave" of the Folio
list of characters should present a credibly grotesque
debasement of physical humanity. Caliban is capable of
not a few human conditions (e.g. lust, drunkenness, and
pleasure in music) so that his appearance, however brutal, must indicate an aspiration towards human nature,
whereas Ariel's is away from it.

With the goddesses the play should reach its peak of
sumptuousness. All three of them are well contrasted in
character and function: Juno, grand, and consummate,
the highest queen of state; rich and bounteous Ceres,
symbol of nature's bounty; and Iris, about whom Shakespeare has virtually written a note to the designer:

> . . . many-color'd messenger. . . .
> Who with thy saffron wings. . . .
>
> (IV.i.76–78)

The ship's crew, and Stephano and Trinculo, present no great problem. They should wear whatever harmonizes with the other costumes and at the same time suggests their professional occupations.

Music plays a very important part in establishing the successive atmospheres of the play. In no other play of Shakespeare is it so organically integrated. If special composition can be afforded, it should be borne in mind, first and foremost, that whoever hears the music of the island is immediately enchanted by it. Purveyors of *musique concrète* are apt to tax an audience's credulity when Caliban speaks of the sounds and *sweet* airs. Certainly the structure of the songs warrants a melodic setting. If, on the other hand, existing music (recorded or live) has to be used, the more recondite ensembles (including harp and/or harpsichord) are likely to provide the most suitable accompaniments. There is so much wonderful early seventeenth-century music that is almost completely unknown that, if the play is being given a contemporary setting, producers need look no further.

CHARACTERS AND CASTING

Prospero

Prospero so dominates the play both in length and dramatic function that the choice of actor for the part must largely determine the character of the whole production.

In performance the part presents certain hazards. One is a tendency to stress the magician at the expense of the man. This generally results in a delivery of booming tedium and an appearance of minor prophet, with costume and make-up vaguely after William Blake. The intention is to match the great hieratic moments, but these are only effective if the inner tension of the personal conflict has been first suggested. Sir John Gielgud's performance at Stratford-upon-Avon in 1957 offered an exemplary reassessment of the character. Ascetic, wiry, and middle-aged in appearance, he admirably combined the three identities of father, duke, and magician.

Those who prefer their Prosperos old adduce evidence from the text: "Bear with my weakness; my old brain is troubled" (IV.i.159) and, "Every third thought shall be my grave" (V.i.312). But the first of these remarks is addressed to Ferdinand and Miranda under particularly exacting circumstances. It is a common habit of the older generation to exaggerate its age to the younger. Moreover, Shakespeare's contemporaries regarded fifty and over as older than we do. The second quotation seems even less convincing. Even to a modern quinquagenarian one thought out of three on any topic as absorbing as the grave may not seem unduly excessive.

Another aspect of Prospero which is apt to worry actors, producers, and, in consequence, the audience, is his puritanism. The puritanism of *The Tempest* is similar to that of *Comus*. That is to say, it is both positive and idealistic. Its frankest and fullest expression occurs in Prospero's adjurations to Ferdinand before the Masque:

> If thou dost break her virgin knot before
> All sanctimonious ceremonies may
> With full and holy rite be minister'd
> No sweet aspersion shall the heavens let fall
> To make this contract grow . . .   (IV.i.15–19)

and again:

> Look thou be true; do not give dalliance
> Too much the rein: the strongest oaths are straw
> To the fire i' the blood: be more abstemious,
> Or else, good night your vow.   (IV.i.51–54)

To both these injunctions, Ferdinand replies with prompt

and ardent acquiescence. The modern error is to present this kind of feeling in the spirit of Thou Shalt Not. There is no space here to go into the spiritual background of the Renaissance ideal of chastity. It must suffice to say that Shakespeare in *The Tempest* is writing in full accord with that ideal. Nowadays our attitude to the matter is supposedly more pragmatic. But in the seventeenth century glandular determinism did not enjoy the cultural ascendancy it does today.

If Prospero's sacramental attitude to sex can be presented as a thing of joy and love rather than as the restrictive suspiciousness of a prurient *voyeur,* then it should be dramatically acceptable to all who can respond to the imaginative presentation of ideas different from their own.

"The Lords"

Thus theatrical parlance has named them, and, on the whole, disparagingly. Most actors regard them as unrewarding parts. Yet they are all (even Adrian and Francisco) firmly characterized. Their superficial penalty as parts is that they seem to begin much better than they finish. Antonio and Sebastian, for instance, say very little in the last two acts, and Alonso's and Gonzalo's best scenes occur before the last act. Yet the play requires that these characters become increasingly passive with the approach of the denouement. Viewed as deliberate rather than casual, this tapering of individuation may seem a dramatic advantage if the actors concerned will play their later silences and responses for what they are worth.

More often than not the parts are undercast. What, above all, they must have is an aristocratic quality. If the implicit assumption that what they say and do and think carries public consequences is lacking, then indeed, they are insufficient strands in the play's texture. Given this quality, however, they are all good parts, and will repay vigilant interpretation.

Alonso develops most. Beginning as an accessory before the fact of Antonio's usurpation, he subsequently shows that the roots of evil do not lie deep in his nature. A sense of bereavement numbs him into frigid isolation. The kindly solicitude of Gonzalo merely jars upon his nerves:

> You cram these words into mine ears, against
> The stomach of my sense . . .   (II.i.111–12)

Then, increasing awareness of the quality of the island revives his hopes until the indictment of the banquet scene brings him his purgation. It is a sign of the importance Shakespeare attaches to this moment that he gives Alonso one of the greatest speeches in the play:

> O, it is monstrous, monstrous!
> Methought the billows spoke and told me of it;
> The winds did sing it to me, and the thunder,
> That deep and dreadful organ pipe, pronounced
> The name of Prosper: it did bass my trespass.
>   (III.iii.95–99)

From this moment he is ready for arraignment and acquittal. Shakespeare adds sympathetic touches to the portrait right up to the end. There is the poignant honesty of:

> But, O, how oddly will it sound that I
> Must ask my child forgiveness!   (V.i.197–98)

An even more delicate moment comes a little later. It falls to Gonzalo to invoke divine blessing on the betrothal of the lovers, and then his sovereign quietly adds: "I say, Amen, Gonzalo" (V.i.204). The humility of that echo is conclusive guarantee of Alonso's regeneration.

Both Sebastian and Antonio are established with brilliant clarity.[1] What a wealth of characterization, for instance, there is in Sebastian's:

---

[1] W. H. Auden's *The Sea and the Mirror* is perhaps nowhere more perceptive and illuminating than in its portraits of Antonio and Sebastian.

>   to ebb
>   Hereditary sloth instructs me
>   (II.i.226–27)

with its overtones of decadent complacency and passive
arrogance. He is the perfect victim for Antonio's strength
and eloquence. Nor is Antonio's power over him broken
at the end. "What things are these, my Lord Antonio?"
(V.i.264), with its blustering flippancy, expressive of the
man's discomfiture but also of his impenitence, tells us
that Antonio is not the only younger brother who Shakespeare leaves unredeemed. The strength of Antonio's will
and the weakness of Sebastian's are what raise their re-
spective resistances to the possibility of spiritual growth.

Gonzalo is a more conventionally drawn character. If,
in addition to suggesting the warmth and humor of the
man, the actor can match Shakespeare's audacity in allowing him every now and again to slip over the edge of
tedium (to his companions, of course, not to the audience), then the part becomes a valuable and restful
element in the total composition.

Ferdinand and Miranda

The contemporary theatrical climate is not conducive
to the breeding of Shakespeare's golden lads and girls.
There is a marked deficiency in young actors and actresses
who can encompass the poetic, physical, and social qualities without which such parts become otiose. Yet, when
they are well played, both parts emerge with charm and
vitality. Miranda is alive and individual from the breath-
less anxiety of her opening speech. She is never afraid—
for all her delicacy of mind—of expressing her feelings,
and this candor of soul reaches an exquisite climax with
her famous exclamation on first seeing the royal visitors

>   O, wonder!
>   How many goodly creatures are there here!
>   How beauteous mankind is! O brave new world,
>   That has such people in 't!   (V.i.181–84)

And, although her father, with his gentle aside, is not slow to point out the irony of her observation, for a moment the audience will do right to see the world through Miranda's eyes. (It seldom happens like this, however, as the speech invariably raises a laugh in the theater, a depressing reflection on the chances of a reasonable hearing for idealism.)

Ferdinand is a prince charming worthy of such a paragon. Courage, rapture, and nobility are written into the part with enough dramatic *raison d'être* for the right sort of actor to make him a real person as well.

Ariel and Caliban

Ariel is probably the most difficult part in the play to cast satisfactorily. The sheer spirituality of the character puts it beyond the range of most actors (and further still beyond actresses). Add to this the need for extreme physical mobility and grace, a highly developed vocal technique both in speaking and singing, and it is clear that the demands of the part are indeed difficult to meet. Yet the problem of casting Ariel and Caliban is not made easier by the tendency to conceive both characters in terms that are vague and sentimental. For Ariel this involves overtones of Peter Pan, and for Caliban that of Our Dumb Friends' League.

Perhaps it is a mistake to approach either character in terms solely of itself. In fact, I find it difficult to think of either of them apart from Prospero, and believe that they only make full imaginative sense if apprehended as externalized aspects of Prospero—the one of his spiritual, the other of his sensual appetencies. The conditions of earthly existence do not permit either of these appetencies to overreach themselves, or gratify themselves at the expense of one another, without some injury to the total organism of the self; in this way, the violence of some of Prospero's encounters with both his servants may find its aptest dramatic manifestation in terms of some such symbol of tension. Moreover, both Ariel and Caliban acquire, at certain moments, phenomenal accesses of energy, and these always occur in sight of their own particular horizon of liberation. "What shall I do? say what? what shall I do?" cries Ariel after Prospero has promised to discharge him within two days; and we should feel there is no limit for the answer. Correspondingly Caliban's "Freedom, high-day, high-day freedom, freedom, high-day, freedom" is nothing if not the natural and exultant expression of the brute instinct glorying in its sudden discovery of independent vitality, when the social inhibitions laid upon it by authority have been released by alcohol.

It is, of course, very difficult, perhaps impossible, to suggest such ultimately abstract notions at all *specifically* on the stage. But one can suggest their *possibility*. That is to say, the appeal must be made to the imagination rather than to the intellect. One cannot be too careful about introducing such notions into the overall concept of a production, but if such a triune relationship as I have indicated can be encompassed—and it can certainly be *assisted* by discreet costuming as well as casting—then I am sure it can only enhance the extraordinarily powerful impression which the supernatural element in the play is capable of making.

Stephano and Trinculo

Here, again, the watch must be set up against mawkishness, without sacrificing any of the comic opportunities. Both characters are firmly integrated in the subplot, and this involves them in a program the items of which include rape and murder. Though their plan is abjectly mismanaged, it is still a serious project, and brings out the worst in both of them. Stephano's domination over Trinculo echoes, in cruder terms, Antonio's over Sebastian. His immediate reactions to all predicaments are selfish, greedy, and unimaginative. Of all Shakespeare's drunkards, he is the least acquainted with delight. His apology to Trinculo is the only generous action he performs, and that is hardly disinterested.

With the possible exception of Malvolio, Trinculo is the most neurotic of Shakespeare's comic characters. His stage life is a progress from fear to fear, beginning with the weather. His mind is more sensitive than Stephano's, but its only introductions are to terror and misery. The decadence of the Neapolitan court could receive no more conclusive attestation than when its jester and its butler are rejected by the sea.

Suggested References

The number of possible references is vast and grows alarmingly. (The *Shakespeare Quarterly* devotes a substantial part of one issue each year to a list of the previous year's work, and *Shakespeare Survey*—an annual publication—includes a substantial review of recent scholarship, as well as an occasional essay surveying a few decades of scholarship on a chosen topic.) Though no works are indispensable, those listed below have been found helpful.

1. Shakespeare's Times

Byrne, M. St. Clare. *Elizabethan Life in Town and Country*. Rev. ed. New York: Barnes & Noble, Inc., 1961. Chapters on manners, beliefs, education, etc., with illustrations.

Craig, Hardin. *The Enchanted Glass: the Elizabethan Mind in Literature*. New York and London: Oxford University Press, 1936. The Elizabethan intellectual climate.

Nicoll, Allardyce (ed.). *The Elizabethans*. London: Cambridge University Press, 1957. An anthology of Elizabethan writings, especially valuable for its illustrations from paintings, title pages, etc.

Shakespeare's England. 2 vols. Oxford: The Clarendon Press, 1916. A large collection of scholarly essays on a wide variety of topics (e.g., astrology, costume, gardening, horsemanship), with special attention to Shakespeare's references to these topics.

Tillyard, E. M. W. *The Elizabethan World Picture.* London: Chatto & Windus, 1943; New York: The Macmillan Company, 1944. A brief account of some Elizabethan ideas of the universe.

Wilson, John Dover (ed.). *Life in Shakespeare's England.* 2nd ed. New York: The Macmillan Company, 1913. An anthology of Elizabethan writings on the countryside, superstition, education, the court, etc.

2. Shakespeare

Bentley, Gerald E. *Shakespeare: A Biographical Handbook.* New Haven, Conn.: Yale University Press, 1961. The facts about Shakespeare, with virtually no conjecture intermingled.

Bradby, Anne (ed.). *Shakespeare Criticism, 1919–1935.* London: Oxford University Press, 1936. A small anthology of excellent essays on the plays.

Bush, Geoffrey Douglas. *Shakespeare and the Natural Condition.* Cambridge, Mass.: Harvard University Press; London: Oxford University Press, 1956. A short, sensitive account of Shakespeare's view of "Nature," touching most of the works.

Chambers, E. K. *William Shakespeare: A Study of Facts and Problems.* 2 vols. London: Oxford University Press, 1930. An invaluable, detailed reference work; not for the casual reader.

Chute, Marchette. *Shakespeare of London.* New York: E. P. Dutton & Co., Inc., 1949. A readable biography fused with portraits of Stratford and London life.

Clemen, Wolfgang H. *The Development of Shakespeare's Imagery.* Cambridge, Mass.: Harvard University Press, 1951. (Originally published in German, 1936.) A temperate account of a subject often abused.

Craig, Hardin. *An Interpretation of Shakespeare*. Columbia, Mo.: Lucas Brothers, 1948. A scholar's book designed for the layman. Comments on all the works.

Dean, Leonard F. (ed.). *Shakespeare: Modern Essays in Criticism*. New York: Oxford University Press, 1957. Mostly mid-twentieth-century critical studies, covering Shakespeare's artistry.

Granville-Barker, Harley. *Prefaces to Shakespeare*. 2 vols. Princeton, N.J.: Princeton University Press, 1946–47. Essays on ten plays by a scholarly man of the theater.

Harbage, Alfred. *As They Liked It*. New York: The Macmillan Company, 1947. A sensitive, long essay on Shakespeare, morality, and the audience's expectations.

Ridler, Anne Bradby (ed.). *Shakespeare Criticism, 1935–1960*. New York and London: Oxford University Press, 1963. An excellent continuation of the anthology edited earlier by Miss Bradby (see above.).

Smith, D. Nichol (ed.). *Shakespeare Criticism*. New York: Oxford University Press, 1916. A selection of criticism from 1623 to 1840, ranging from Ben Jonson to Thomas Carlyle.

Spencer, Theodore. *Shakespeare and the Nature of Man*. New York: The Macmillan Company, 1942. Shakespeare's plays in relation to Elizabethan thought.

Stoll, Elmer Edgar. *Shakespeare and Other Masters*. Cambridge, Mass.: Harvard University Press; London: Oxford University Press, 1940. Essays on tragedy, comedy, and aspects of dramaturgy, with special reference to some of Shakepeare's plays.

Traversi, D. A. *An Approach to Shakespeare*. Rev. ed. New York: Doubleday & Co., Inc., 1956. An analysis of the plays, beginning with words, images, and themes, rather than with characters.

Van Doren, Mark. *Shakespeare*. New York: Henry Holt & Company, Inc., 1939. Brief, perceptive readings of all of the plays.

Whitaker, Virgil K. *Shakespeare's Use of Learning*. San Marino, Calif.: Huntington Library, 1953. A study of the relation of Shakespeare's reading to his development as a dramatist.

3. Shakespeare's Theater

Adams, John Cranford. *The Globe Playhouse*. Rev. ed. New York: Barnes & Noble, Inc., 1961. A detailed conjecture about the physical characteristics of the theater Shakespeare often wrote for.

Beckerman, Bernard. *Shakespeare at the Globe, 1599–1609*. New York: The Macmillan Company, 1962. On the playhouse and on Elizabethan dramaturgy, acting, and staging.

Chambers, E. K. *The Elizabethan Stage*. 4 vols. New York: Oxford University Press, 1923. Reprinted with corrections, 1945. An indispensable reference work on theaters, theatrical companies, and staging at court.

Harbage, Alfred. *Shakespeare's Audience*. New York: Columbia University Press; London: Oxford University Press, 1941. A study of the size and nature of the theatrical public.

Hodges, C. Walter. *The Globe Restored*. London: Ernest Benn, Ltd., 1953; New York: Coward-McCann, Inc., 1954. A well-illustrated and readable attempt to reconstruct the Globe Theatre.

Nagler, A. M. *Shakespeare's Stage*. Tr. by Ralph Manheim. New Haven, Conn.: Yale University Press, 1958. An excellent brief introduction to the physical aspect of the playhouse.

Smith, Irwin. *Shakespeare's Globe Playhouse*. New York: Charles Scribner's Sons, 1957. Chiefly indebted to J. C. Adams' controversial book, with additional material and scale drawings for model-builders.

Venezky, Alice S. *Pageantry on the Shakespearean Stage*. New York: Twayne Publishers, Inc., 1951. An examination of spectacle in Elizabethan drama.

4. Miscellaneous Reference Works

Abbott, E. A. *A Shakespearean Grammar*. New edition. New York: The Macmillan Company, 1877. An examination of differences between Elizabethan and modern grammar.

Bartlett, John. *A New and Complete Concordance . . . to . . . Shakespeare*. New York: The Macmillan Company, 1894. An index to most of Shakespeare's words.

Bullough, Geoffrey. *Narrative and Dramatic Sources of Shakespeare*. 4 vols. Vols. 5 and 6 in preparation. New York: Columbia University Press; London: Routledge & Kegan Paul, Ltd., 1957–. A collection of many of the books Shakespeare drew upon.

Greg, W. W. *The Shakespeare First Folio*. New York and London: Oxford University Press, 1955. A detailed yet readable history of the first collection (1623) of Shakespeare's plays.

Kökeritz, Helge. *Shakespeare's Names*. New Haven, Conn.: Yale University Press, 1959; London: Oxford University Press, 1960. A guide to the pronunciation of some 1,800 names appearing in Shakespeare.

———. *Shakespeare's Pronunciation*. New Haven, Conn.: Yale University Press; London: Oxford University Press, 1953. Contains much information about puns and rhymes.

Linthicum, Marie C. *Costume in the Drama of Shakespeare and His Contemporaries*. New York and London: Oxford University Press, 1936. On the fabrics and dress of the age, and references to them in the plays.

Muir, Kenneth. *Shakespeare's Sources*. London: Methuen & Co., Ltd., 1957. Vol. 2 in preparation. The first volume, on the comedies and tragedies, attempts to ascertain what books were Shakespeare's sources, and what use he made of them.

Onions, C. T. *A Shakespeare Glossary*. London: Oxford University Press, 1911; 2nd ed., rev., with enlarged addenda, 1953. Definitions of words (or senses of words) now obsolete.

Partridge, Eric. *Shakespeare's Bawdy*. Rev. ed. New York: E. P. Dutton & Co., Inc.; London: Routledge & Kegan Paul, Ltd., 1955. A glossary of bawdy words and phrases.

Shakespeare Quarterly. See headnote to Suggested References.

Shakespeare Survey. See headnote to Suggested References.

Smith, Gordon Ross. *A Classified Shakespeare Bibliography 1936–1958*. University Park, Pa.: Pennsylvania State University Press, 1963. A list of some 20,000 items on Shakespeare.

5. The Tempest

Auden, W. H. "The Sea and the Mirror: A Commentary on Shakespeare's *The Tempest*," *The Collected Poetry*. New York: Random House, Inc., 1945.

———. *The Dyer's Hand and Other Essays*. London: Faber & Faber, Ltd.; New York: Random House, Inc., 1962, pp. 128–34, 524–27.

Gilbert, Allan H. *"The Tempest:* Parallelism in Characters and Situations," *The Journal of English and Germanic Philology,* XIV (1915), 63–74.

Hazlitt, William. *"The Tempest," Characters of Shakespear's Plays,* 1817. Reprinted in *The Round Table* [*and*] *Characters of Shakespear's Plays,* London: J. M. Dent & Sons, Ltd.; New York: E. P. Dutton & Co., Inc., 1957 (Everyman's Library).

James, David G. "The Failure of the Ballad-Makers," *Scepticism and Poetry*. London: Allen & Unwin, Ltd., 1937; New York: Barnes & Noble, Inc., 1960.

Knight, G. Wilson. *The Crown of Life*. New York and London: Oxford University Press, 1947.

———. *The Shakespearian Tempest*. New York and London: Oxford University Press, 1932.

Leavis, F. R. "The Criticism of Shakespeare's Late Plays," *The Common Pursuit*. London: Chatto & Windus, Ltd., 1952; Harmondsworth, Eng.: Penguin Books, Ltd., 1962.

Murry, John Middleton. *Shakespeare*. London: Jonathan Cape, Ltd.; New York: Harcourt, Brace & Company, Inc., 1936.

Spencer, Theodore. "Appearance and Reality in Shakespeare's Last Plays," *Modern Philology,* XXXIX (1942), 265–74.

Still, Colin. *Shakespeare's Mystery Play: A Study of "The Tempest."* London: Cecil Palmer, 1921. Revised as *The Timeless Theme*. London: Nicholson & Watson, Ltd., 1936.

Strachey, Lytton. "Shakespeare's Final Period," *Books and Characters*. London: Chatto & Windus, Ltd.; New York: Harcourt, Brace & Company, Inc., 1922. Reprinted in *Literary Essays*. London: Chatto & Windus, Ltd., 1948; New York: Harcourt, Brace & Company, Inc., 1949.

Tillyard, E. M. W. *Shakespeare's Last Plays*. London: Chatto & Windus, Ltd., 1938. Part of the material on *The Tempest* is reprinted above.

Traversi, Derek A. *Shakespeare: The Last Phase*. New York: Harcourt, Brace & Company, Inc., 1955; London: Hollis & Carter, Ltd., 1954.

Wilson, J. Dover. *The Meaning of "The Tempest."* Robert Spence Watson Memorial Lecture, published by the Literary and Philosophical Society of Newcastle upon Tyne, 1936.